SALVETE!

A FIRST COURSE IN LATIN
BOOK ONE

Ed and
Mary Catherine Phinney

University of Massachusetts at Amherst, U.S.A.

CAMBRIDGE
UNIVERSITY PRESS

PUBLISHED BY THE PRESS SYNDICATE OF THE UNIVERSITY OF CAMBRIDGE
The Pitt Building, Trumpington Street, Cambridge CB2 1RP, United Kingdom

CAMBRIDGE UNIVERSITY PRESS
The Edinburgh Building, Cambridge CB2 2RU, UK   http://www.cup.cam.ac.uk
40 West 20th Street, New York, NY 10011-4211, USA   http://www.cup.org
10 Stamford Road, Oakleigh, Melbourne 3166, Australia

This edition first published 1995
Reprinted 1998

Printed in the United States of America

Library of Congress Cataloguing-in-Publication Data applied for

ISBN 0-521-40683-8 paperback

Drawings by Rodney Sutton
Maps by Chris E. Etheridge
Cover illustration by Hemesh Alles
Picture research by Callie Kendall

Acknowledgements
Thanks are due to the following for permission to reproduce photographs: 41, Tourist
Information, Detmond; 46, Chris Payne/Life File; 61*t*, Mike Adnrews/Ancient Art &
Architecture Collection; 61*b*, Ronald Sheridan/Ancient Art & Architecture Collection

Contents

CHAPTER I familia Rōmāna

In the ancient city of Rome, in A.D. 9, lived a successful businessman named Rubrius. His house was located on the Quirinal hill on the northwestern side of the city. The Quirinal is one of the seven hills on which Rome was built.

Rubrius' family was quite large and included members whom we today might not consider to be part of the family.

1 Model Sentences

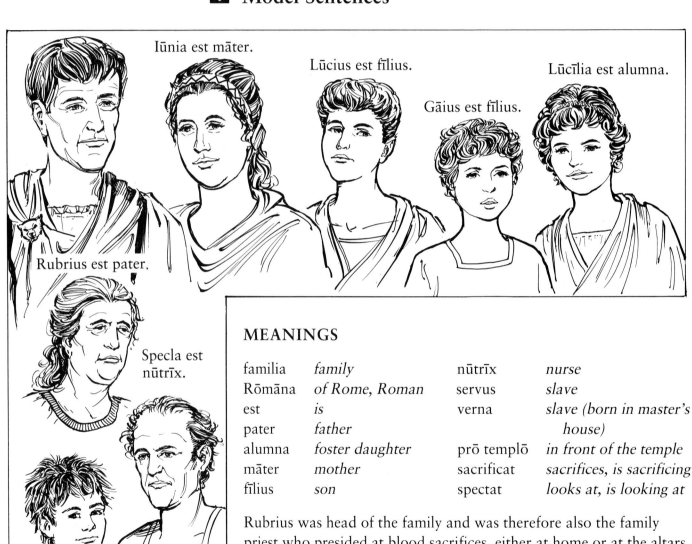

Iūnia est māter.

Lūcius est fīlius.

Lūcīlia est alumna.

Gāius est fīlius.

Rubrius est pater.

Specla est nūtrīx.

Celtillus est servus.

Cernunnus est verna.

MEANINGS

familia	*family*	nūtrīx	*nurse*
Rōmāna	*of Rome, Roman*	servus	*slave*
est	*is*	verna	*slave (born in master's house)*
pater	*father*		
alumna	*foster daughter*	prō templō	*in front of the temple*
māter	*mother*	sacrificat	*sacrifices, is sacrificing*
fīlius	*son*	spectat	*looks at, is looking at*

Rubrius was head of the family and was therefore also the family priest who presided at blood sacrifices, either at home or at the altars located outside temples. Sacrifices were like meals to which the gods were invited as spiritual guests. The gods' portion of meat was burned on the altar, and wine was poured on the flames at the same time. The meat usually came from domesticated animals like cattle, sheep, goats, or pigs.

pater est prō templō.
pater prō templō sacrificat.

māter est prō templō.
māter prō templō spectat.

2 sacrificium

Minerva in templō stat. Rubrius prō templō sacrificat. Iūnia intentē
spectat. Lūcius adiuvat. Lūcīlia adiuvat. Gāius sūrsum deorsum salit.
Gāius est pestis. pater est īrātus, sed pater tacet. pater prō templō
sacrificat.

MEANINGS

sacrificium	*a, the sacrifice*
Minerva	*Roman goddess of war and crafts*
in templō	*in a, the temple, in her temple*
stat	*stands, is standing*
sacrificat	*sacrifices, is sacrificing*
intentē	*intently*
spectat	*looks at, is looking at*
adiuvat	*helps, is helping*
sūrsum deorsum	*up and down*
salit	*jumps, is jumping*
pestis	*pest, rascal, nuisance*
īrātus	*angry*
sed	*but*
tacet	*is silent, is quiet*

PATTERNS

1 Latin does not have special words for "a" or "the." Supply these in English as the sense of the story demands. For example:

pater tacet.
Father is quiet.
Or: *The father is quiet.*
Or: *A father is quiet.*

2 Translate each of the following sentences in the three ways shown above:

1 nūtrīx intentē spectat.
2 alumna prō templō stat.
3 māter tacet.

Roman elementary schools were private, usually held in single rooms in poor and crowded parts of the city. There was normally one teacher per school, and he was often a slave. He taught reading, writing, and arithmetic. The school year began after March 23, which was a holiday (the **Quīnquātrūs**) honoring Minerva, the goddess celebrated for her learning and wisdom.

3 in lūdō

magister est in lūdō. magister in lūdō sedet. Gāius est in lūdō. Gāius nōn sedet. Gāius sūrsum deorsum salit. magister est īrātus. magister clāmat, "sedē, pestis!"

MEANINGS

in lūdō	*in school*
magister	*master, teacher*
sedet	*sits, is sitting*
nōn	*not*
sūrsum deorsum	*up and down*
salit	*jumps, is jumping*
īrātus	*angry*
clāmat	*shouts*
sedē!	*sit!*
pestis	*pest, rascal*

PATTERNS

1 Latin verbs have different endings. Forms like **est** and **sedet** can only be used to tell about single individuals or things:

> māter **est** īrāta *Mother (the mother, a mother)* **is** *angry.*
> Not: *Mother* **are** *angry.*
> magister **sedet**. *The teacher (teacher, a teacher)* **is sitting down.**
> Not: *The teacher* **are sitting down.**

2 Study the endings of the following verbs, and then say which part of the verb shows that it is talking about "he," "she," or "it:"

> clāmat, sedet, est, stat, tacet, adiuvat, spectat, salit.

3 Translate the following sentences into English:

> 1 Gāius in lūdō nōn sedet.
> 2 Gāius sūrsum deorsum salit.
> 3 Lūcīlia in lūdō sedet.
> 4 Lūcīlia est īrāta.

Cloth for ordinary Roman clothes was usually woven at home by women of the family, both slaves and free women. The cloth was woven on an upright loom made of two posts joined by a beam set on top of them.

4 in cubiculō

Specla in cubiculō stat. Specla texit. Iūnia in cubiculō sedet. Iūnia suit. Lūcīlia in cubiculō sedet. Lūcīlia quoque suit. Specla texit et cantat. Iūnia suit et cantat. Lūcīlia nōn cantat. Lūcīlia difficulter suit.

MEANINGS

in cubiculō	*in a, the bedroom*
stat	*stands, is standing*
texit	*weaves, is weaving*
suit	*sews, is sewing*
quoque	*also*
et	*and*
cantat	*sings, is singing*
nōn	*not*
difficulter	*with difficulty*

Like many ancient Romans, Rubrius enjoyed blood sports. He particularly liked the bouts between gladiators who fought to the death in the arena of the oval-shaped building called the amphitheater. To provide variety for the show, gladiators were armed in different ways: some with body armor, others without body armor, but both groups with sword and shield; some nearly naked with only a large fork (called a trident) and a net to defend themselves with. Gladiators were usually foreign-born slaves or prisoners of war.

5 in amphitheātrō

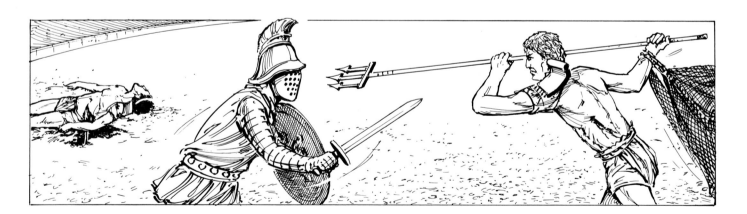

gladiātor in arēnā stat. familia in amphitheātrō sedet et spectat. gladiātor ferōciter pugnat. Cernunnus tacet. Gāius sūrsum deorsum salit. Lūcīlia lacrimat.

Lūcīlia clāmat, "Gāius est pestis!"
gladiātor in arēnā iacet.
"ēheu!" Lūcīlia clāmat, "gladiātor est mortuus." Lūcīlia lacrimat.
"euge!" Gāius clāmat, "gladiātor est mortuus." Gāius salit.
Cernunnus nōn clāmat. Cernunnus nōn salit. Cernunnus tacet.
gladiātor est Gallicus.

MEANINGS

in amphitheātrō	*in an, the amphitheater*
gladiātor	*gladiator*
in arēnā	*in the arena*
stat	*stands, is standing*
familia	*family*
et	*and*
spectat	*looks at, watches, is watching*
ferōciter	*fiercely*
pugnat	*fights, is fighting*
tacet	*is silent, is quiet*
sūrsum deorsum	*up and down*
salit	*is jumping, jumps*
lacrimat	*is crying, cries*
clāmat	*shouts*
pestis!	*pest!, rascal!*
iacet	*lies, is lying*
ēheu!	*oh dear!*
mortuus	*dead*
euge!	*hurrah!*
Gallicus	*Gallic, Gaulish, from Gaul*

Key Words

1 Do you remember the meanings of the following words? If not, write the words on a piece of paper, look up their meanings above or in the **Complete Word Meanings** (pp. 70–5), write them out, and memorize them.

nouns	*adjectives*	*verbs*
fīlius	īrātus	cantat
gladiātor	īrāta	clāmat
magister		salit
māter		sedet
pater		spectat
		stat
		tacet

2 Choose one word from each of the three lists above and make a three-word sentence. Be sure to keep the order of the lists. Write the sentence out on a piece of paper. Continue like this until you have written as many sensible sentences as you can, and then translate them.

3 Find the Latin parent words in the **Key Words** above for the following English words: chant, claim, irate, magistrate, maternity, paternal, sediment, spectacular, stable, taciturn.

Look up the meaning of each English word (if you do not already know it) and then explain how the meaning of the parent word is connected to the meaning of the English word (derivative).

CHAPTER II laetitia

The English word *paedagogue* usually denotes a schoolteacher. But the Roman **paedagōgus** was an adult slave charged with looking after the family's freeborn children, especially while they were going to and returning from school. Slave children did not attend school.

6 Model Sentences

paedagōgus tabulam portat.

Gāius stilum habet.

magister chartam habet.

Lūcīlia tabulam habet.

MEANINGS

laetitia	*joy*
paedagōgus	*slave (in charge of school-age children)*
tabulam	*(waxed board) writing tablet*
portat	*carries, is carrying*
magister	*teacher*
chartam	*a sheet of papyrus, a piece of paper*
habet	*has*
stilum	*stylus*

Schoolchildren wrote their lessons on a special board, made of thickly waxed wood. They pressed their letters into the wax with a stylus, or stick.

7 magister īrātus

magister in lūdō ambulat.

Lūcīlia scrībit. magister tabulam īnspicit. Lūcīlia rēctē scrībit. magister Lūcīliam laudat.

Gāius scrībit. magister tabulam īnspicit. Gāius nōn rēctē scrībit. magister Gāium nōn laudat.

Gāius est īrātus. Gāius Lūcīliam pulsat. Lūcīlia est īrāta. magister quoque est īrātus. magister Gāium verberat. Gāius sūrsum deorsum salit.

MEANINGS

magister	*teacher*
īrātus	*angry*
in lūdō	*in the school*
ambulat	*walks, is walking*
scrībit	*writes, is writing*
tabulam	*(waxed board) writing tablet*
īnspicit	*inspects, examines*
rēctē	*correctly*
laudat	*praises*
pulsat	*hits*
īrāta	*angry*
quoque	*also*
verberat	*whips*

PATTERNS

1 In Latin, a single person or thing that is the direct object of an action verb has a position different from the one in English:

Gāius **Lūcīliam** pulsat.   *Gaius hits **Lucilia**.*
Lūcīlia **Gāium** pulsat.   *Lucilia hits **Gaius**.*

2 Study the endings of the following singular nouns, and then say which part of the noun marks it as the direct object of an action verb:

tabulam, chartam, stilum, Lūcīliam, Gāium.

3 Translate the following sentences into English:

1 Gāius Lūcīliam pulsat.
2 Lūcīlia Gāium nōn laudat.
3 Gāius tabulam habet.

A Roman tavern was essentially a store, but the Roman taverns that sold wine would have resembled a modern tavern. Customers at a wine tavern used to sit on stools around a table and drink their wine from cups. The store-owner kept his supply of wine in gigantic clay storage jars called **amphorae**.

8 in tabernā

paedagōgus nōn est in lūdō. paedagōgus in tabernā stat. paedagōgus vīnum bibit et cantat. paedagōgus est laetus.

Rubrius tabernam intrat. Rubrius vīnum nōn bibit. Rubrius paedagōgum videt. Rubrius est īrātus et clāmat, "furcifer!" Rubrius paedagōgum ad lūdum dūcit.

MEANINGS

in tabernā	*in a, the tavern*
paedagōgus	*slave (in charge of school-age children)*
in lūdō	*in school*
vīnum	*wine*
bibit	*drinks, is drinking*
laetus	*happy*
tabernam	*tavern*
intrat	*enters*
videt	*sees*
furcifer!	*scoundrel!*
ad	*to*
lūdum	*school*
dūcit	*leads*

PATTERNS

1 Study the following sentences and their translations:

Iūnia **clāmat**	*Iunia shouts.*
clāmat.	*She shouts.*
paedagōgus **cantat.**	*The paedagogus (a paedagogus, paedagogus) is singing.*
cantat.	*He is singing.*

The **-t** in **clāma*t*** and **canta*t*** by itself means "she," "he," or "it." In English, when the "she," "he," or "it" is named, we use the name and leave out the "he," "she," or "it."

2 Translate the following sentences:

1 Gāius nōn scrībit.
2 nōn scrībit.
3 magister clāmat.
4 clāmat.
5 Lūcīlia rēctē scrībit.
6 rēctē scrībit.

Successful gladiators were heroes to many Roman boys, who would have enjoyed imitating them by fighting play duels with sticks. In their training schools, the gladiators themselves used wooden swords called **rudēs** for practice.

9 pugna

Gāius est gladiātor. Cernunnus quoque est gladiātor. Gāius gladium
tenet. Cernunnus quoque gladium tenet. Gāius pugnat. Cernunnus
quoque pugnat.

Celtillus fīlium Cernunnum spectat. Celtillus est īrātus. Celtillus
gladium capit. Celtillus clāmat, "mīles sīc pugnat!" et Gāium leviter
pulsat. Gāius est attonitus.

MEANINGS

pugna	*a, the fight*
quoque	*also*
gladium	*sword*
tenet	*holds, is holding*
pugnat	*fights, is fighting*
fīlium	*son*
spectat	*looks at, watches*
capit	*takes, grabs*
mīles	*soldier*
sīc	*thus, (in) this way*
leviter	*lightly*
pulsat	*hits*
attonitus	*surprised*

The Roman father of the family could accept or reject a newborn
member. The baby was placed on the floor at his feet. If the father
picked the baby up, it meant that he acknowledged it as his own.

▮10▮ susceptiō

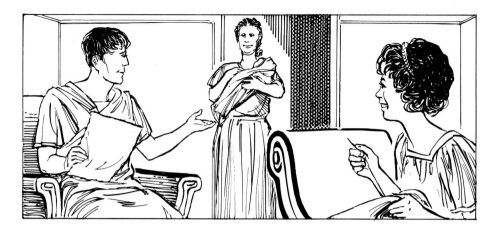

Rubrius in ātriō sedet. Rubrius chartam tenet, sed nōn legit. Lūcīlia in ātriō sedet et suit. ("VAA-AA-AAA! VAA-AA-AAA!") Rubrius rīdet. Lūcīlia quoque rīdet.

  Specla ātrium intrat. nūtrīx īnfantem tenet. nūtrīx īnfantem in pavīmentum pōnit. Rubrius īnfantem spectat. īnfans fortiter vāgit, "VAA-AA-AAA!" Rubrius rīdet. Rubrius īnfantem suscipit. "īnfāns," pater dīcit, "est fīlia mea." īnfāns nōn vāgit. īnfāns tacet.

MEANINGS

susceptiō	*(ritual of) acknowledgement, acceptance*
in ātriō	*in the atrium*
chartam	*a sheet of papyrus, a piece of paper*
tenet	*holds, is holding*
sed	*but*
legit	*reads, is reading*
rīdet	*smiles*
ātrium	*reception room, atrium*
intrat	*enters*
nūtrīx	*nurse*
in pavīmentum	*on the floor*
pōnit	*puts*
spectat	*looks at, watches*
īnfāns	*baby*
fortiter	*loudly*
vāgit	*cries*
suscipit	*picks up*
dīcit	*says*
fīlia	*daughter*
mea	*my*

On the eighth or ninth day after birth, a baby received its name. On this day, the father offered a sacrifice to the gods on the family altar. He then purified the baby by sprinkling water on it in a ceremony similar to that of Christian baptism. Like the present-day baptism in many countries, especially in Italy, the day turned into a big celebration, and relatives would visit, bringing gifts for the newly-named baby.

On this naming day, the father hung a **bulla** around the baby's neck. The bulla was a sacred charm inside a case made of two oval pieces of gold, and shaped rather like an old-fashioned pocket watch. The bulla hung around the baby's neck from a chain or cord.

11 lūstrātiō

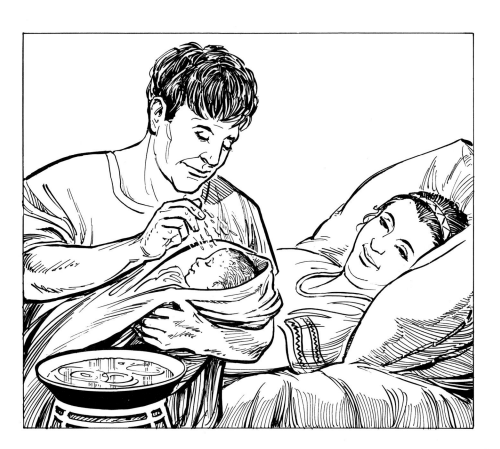

avunculus ātrium intrat. Rubrius avunculum salūtat. amita ātrium intrat. Rubrius amitam quoque salūtat.

pater īnfantem suscipit. pater īnfantem lūstrat. pater mātrem in lectō quoque lūstrat. pater īnfantem tenet et dīcit, "nōmen tuum est Rubria."

nūtrīx Rubriam tenet. Rubria bullam auream gerit. bulla fascinum repellit. īnfāns nunc est tūta.

MEANINGS

lūstrātiō	(ritual of) sprinkling
avunculus	mother's brother, (maternal) uncle
ātrium	reception room, atrium
intrat	enters
salūtat	greets
amita	father's sister, (paternal) aunt
suscipit	picks up
lūstrat	sprinkles
in lectō	on a couch
dīcit	says
nōmen	name
tuum	your
bullam	a protective charm, bulla
auream	made of gold, gold(en)
gerit	wears, is wearing
fascinum	a bewitching stare, the (so-called) "evil eye"
repellit	repels, drives back, keeps away
nunc	now
tūta	safe

PATTERNS

1 Study the following sentences and their translations:

Rubrius in ātriō **stat**.	*Rubrius is standing in the atrium.*
Rubrius īnfantem **tenet**.	*Rubrius is holding the baby.*
Rubrius in ātriō **stat** et īnfantem **tenet**.	*Rubrius is standing in the atrium and is holding the baby.*

Notice how both Latin and English make a long sentence out of two shorter sentences. In the examples above, Rubrius is mentioned in each short sentence, but only once when the two short sentences are put together.

Note: the **-t** ending of the verb tene*t*, meaning "**he** is holding," and also the "is" help remind us that it is **Rubrius** who is holding.

2 Translate the following sentences:

A Cernunnus gladium tenet.   B Cernunnus pugnat.
C Cernunnus gladium tenet et pugnat.

A Celtillus est pater. B Celtillus fīlium adiuvat.
C Celtillus est pater et fīlium adiuvat.

3 On a piece of paper, write a new (C) sentence in Latin, using words from the two previous (A and B) sentences:

A pater prō templō sacrificat. B pater tacet.
C:
A gladiātor in arēnā stat. B gladiātor pugnat.
C:
A gladiātor in arēnā iacet. B gladiātor est mortuus.
C:

12 īnfāns

Specla in cubiculō stat. Specla Rubriam tenet. īnfāns vāgit. nūtrīx suāviter lallat, "LAL-LĀ, LAL-LĀ." īnfāns tacet et dormit.

Lūcīlia in lectō recumbit. Lūcīlia pūpam tenet et suāviter lallat, "LAL-LĀ, LAL-LĀ." pūpa tacet et dormit. mox Lūcīlia quoque dormit. Specla rīdet et exit.

MEANINGS

vāgit	*cries, is crying*
suāviter	*sweetly*
lallat	*sings, is singing a lullaby*
dormit	*sleeps, is sleeping*
in lectō	*on a couch*
recumbit	*lies down, is lying down*
pūpa	*doll*
mox	*soon*
exit	*goes out*

Lullabies

"Lallā, lallā," is part of a Latin lullaby. It recalls similar songs in many languages. In a French lullaby, "lolo" rhymes with "dodo," or "sleep" (like Latin "dormit"):

> Fais dodo,
> Colin mon p'tit frère,
> Fais dodo,
> T'auras du lolo.

In an Old English ballad, "lulla" of "lulla-by" becomes "lullay":

> Lullay, lullay, litel child,
> Softë slep and faste.

Key Words

1

nouns (subjects)	adjective	adverb	nouns (direct objects)	verbs
īnfāns	attonita	suāviter	īnfantem	dormit
nūtrīx			nūtrīcem	habet
				intrat
				scrībit

2 Derivatives: ability, astonished, dormitory, entrance, infantile, nutrition, scribble, sweet.

CHAPTER III fābula

Specla tells Lucilia a story from Hispania (modern Portugal and Spain), where she was born. The story is about a witch with magically powerful eyes.

The ancient Romans, like many other peoples throughout the ages, had their own peculiar superstitions. The most curious was their belief that certain people, particularly old hags, had the power to work magic with their eyes. They thought that these **venēficae**, or "witches," could exercise their power by staring hatefully at their victims. They were said to have the **fascinum**, or "evil eye." They were dangerously "fascinating."

▮13 venēfica

Specla in cubiculō sedet. Lūcīlia quoque in cubiculō sedet. Specla fābulam Hispānicam nārrat:

> venēfica fascinum habet. venēfica in forō ambulat. nūtrīx in forō quoque ambulat. nūtrīx īnfantem tenet. venēfica īnfantem intentē spectat. subitō venēfica īnfantem in mustēlam vertit. nūtrīx clāmat et cum mustēlā domum currit. māter mustēlam videt et clāmat. nūtrīx rem nārrat. māter mustēlam īnspicit. māter deinde bullam in mustēlam pōnit. bulla mustēlam iterum in īnfantem vertit. īnfāns valdē vāgit, sed māter est laeta. nūtrīx quoque est laeta.

MEANINGS

fābula	*story*
venēfica	*hag, witch*
Hispānicam	*Hispanic*

nārrat	*tells*
fascinum	*a bewitching stare, the (so-called) "evil eye"*
in forō	*in the business center, forum*
ambulat	*walks, is walking*
intentē	*intently*
subitō	*suddenly*
in mustēlam	*into a ferret*
vertit	*turns*
cum mustēlā	*with the ferret*
domum	*home(wards)*
currit	*runs*
mustēlam	*ferret*
videt	*sees*
rem nārrat	*tells the story*
īnspicit	*inspects, examines*
deinde	*next, then*
bullam	*a protective charm, bulla*
pōnit	*puts*
iterum	*again*
in īnfantem	*into the baby*
valdē	*much, very much*
sed	*but*
laeta	*happy*

ACTIVITY

Translate all the words below, including those in brackets. Then look at each group of words and choose one of the words in brackets to make a sensible sentence. Translate the completed sentence.

1 magister (tabulam, īnfantem) īnspicit.
2 paedagōgus (stilum, vīnum) bibit.
3 Celtillus (tabernam, gladium) capit.
4 nūtrīx (īnfantem, pavīmentum) tenet.
5 pater (bullam, īnfantem) lūstrat.
6 īnfāns (mustēlam, bullam) gerit.

The seaport of Rome was located near the town of Ostia, some 16 miles away, on the left branch of the Tiber river. In A.D. 9, the harbor was old fashioned and much too small for the rapidly growing commerce of the Roman Empire.

During the early Empire, one of Italy's most popular exports was fine wine. The many varieties of Italian wine were particularly popular in Gaul (France). It was only later that the Gaulish Romans themselves began the cultivation and export of the fine wines for which France is still famous today.

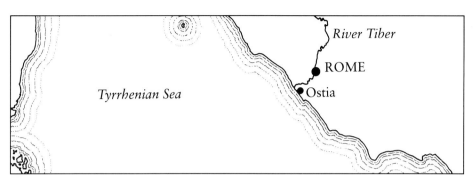

▇14▇ ad portum Ōstiēnsem

Rubrius raedam ad portum Ōstiēnsem hodiē agit. Rubrius portum circumspectat.

"salvē," clāmat magister.

"salvē," respondet Rubrius. Rubrius ē raedā dēscendit. Rubrius horreum videt. servus prō horreō stat et magnam amphoram tenet. amphora multum vīnum continet.

"festīnā, furcifer!" clāmat magister, et servus magnam amphoram in nāvem festīnanter portat. ēheu! servus in aquam incidit.

"oi!" clāmat servus. magister est perterritus et in aquam salit. magister servum ex aquā servat.

servus in nāvem festīnanter cōnscendit. magister in nāvem lentē cōnscendit. Rubrius in raedam cōnscendit et raedam domum agit.

dēnique nāvis est plēna. magister nāvem solvit et ad portum Massiliēnsem nāvigat. nāvis multum vīnum Ītalicum tenet.

MEANINGS

ad portum	*to the port*
Ōstiēnsem	*of Ostia*
raedam	*(four-wheeled) carriage*
hodiē	*today*
agit	*drives*
circumspectat	*looks around*
salvē!	*hello!*
magister	*master (of the ship), captain*
respondet	*answers, replies*
ē raedā	*out of the carriage*
dēscendit	*gets down*
horreum	*storehouse*
videt	*sees*
servus	*slave*
prō horreō	*in front of the storehouse*
magnam	*big*
amphoram	*amphora*
in nāvem	*onto the ship*
multum	*much, lots of*
vīnum	*wine*
continet	*contains*
festīnā!	*hurry!*
festīnanter	*quickly*
furcifer!	*scoundrel!*
portat	*carries*
ēheu!	*oh dear!*
in aquam	*into the water*
incidit	*falls*
oi!	*oh!*
perterritus	*terrified*
ex aquā	*out of the water*
servat	*saves*
cōnscendit	*climbs*
lentē	*slowly*
in raedam	*into the carriage*
domum	*home(wards)*
dēnique	*finally*
nāvis	*ship*
plēna	*full*
nāvem solvit	*sets sail*
Massiliēnsem	*of Massilia (Marseille, France)*
nāvigat	*sails*
Ītalicum	*of Italy, from Italy, Italian*

ACTIVITY

Translate all the words below, including the phrases in brackets. Then look at each group of words and choose one of the phrases in brackets to make a sensible sentence. Translate the completed sentence.

1 magister tabulam (in lūdō, in tabernā) īnspicit.
2 Rubrius paedagōgum (ad tabernam, ad lūdum) dūcit.
3 Rubria (in templō, in pavīmentō) iacet.
4 servus (in aquam, in mustēlam) incidit.
5 venēfica īnfantem (in bullam, in mustēlam) vertit.

The imperial palace of Augustus was built on the north side of the Palatine hill. The Palatine is one of the seven hills on which Rome is built. It overlooked the Forum, the religious and civic center of Rome. Augustus' palace was actually a cluster of buildings. The later Palatine building, or **Palātium**, built by the Emperor Domitian (A.D. 81–96), was so grand that its name has become the general English word for a very large house, a "palace."

15 prope Palātium I

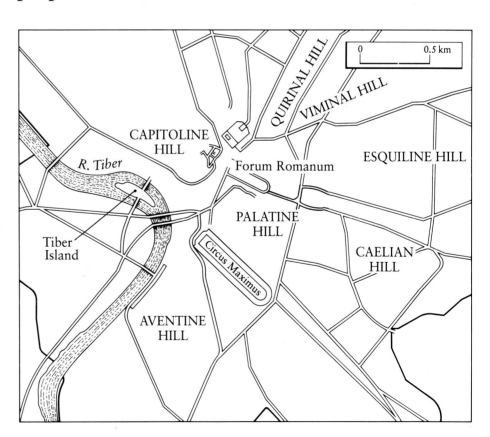

Rubrius ad mercātum equitat. Lūcius ad mercātum quoque equitat. Celtillus plaustrum agit, et Cernunnus iūxtā plaustrum currit. "ecce Palātium!" clāmat Gāius. "ecce domus Augustāna!"

"domus Augustāna marmorea est omnis!" clāmat Lūcius.

"Caesar Augustus, imperātor noster, est bonus et magnus," inquit Rubrius. "pāx iam diū dūrat."

magna turba est in viā. subitō lectīca splendida obstat. Celtillus est īrātus. Cernunnus praecursōrem Aegyptium prō lectīcā splendidā videt.

"exī!" clāmat Cernunnus.

"exī et tū, galle Gallice!" clāmat praecursor Aegyptius.

"ego tamen nōn sum servus Aegyptius," arroganter respondet verna Cernunnus.

MEANINGS

prope Palātium	*near the Palatine hill*
mercātum	*market*
equitat	*rides (a horse), is riding*
plaustrum	*wagon*
agit	*drives, is driving*
iūxtā	*next to, beside*
currit	*runs, is running*
ecce!	*look!*
Palātium	*Palatine hill*
domus	*house*
Augustāna	*of Augustus*
marmorea	*made of marble*
omnis	*entire(ly)*
Caesar Augustus	*Caesar Augustus*
imperātor	*Emperor*
noster	*our*
bonus	*good*
magnus	*big, great*
inquit	*says*
pāx	*peace*
iam diū	*now for a long time*
dūrat	*has endured, lasted*
magna	*big, great*
turba	*crowd*
in viā	*in the street*

MEANINGS

subitō	*suddenly*
lectīca	*portable couch, lectica*
splendida	*splendid, gleaming*
obstat	*blocks the way, is blocking the way*
praecursōrem	*forerunner*
Aegyptium	*of Egypt, from Egypt, Egyptian*
prō lectīcā splendidā	*in front of the splendid lectica*
exī!	*get out!*
et	*too, also*
tū	*you (singular)*
galle!	*rooster!*
Gallice!	*Gallic!, Gaulish!*
Aegyptius	*of Egypt, from Egypt, Egyptian*
ego	*I*
tamen	*however*
sum	*am*
arroganter	*arrogantly*
respondet	*answers, replies*
verna	*slave (born in master's house)*

PATTERNS

1 Study the following direct quotations:

"Gāius est fīlius," Rubrius **dīcit**.
"Gaius is my son," Rubrius says.

"Gāius est fīlius," **dīcit** Rubrius.
"Gaius is my son," says Rubrius.

"Gāius est fīlius," **inquit** Rubrius.
"Gaius is my son," says Rubrius.

Cernunnus **respondet**, "ego sum verna Gallicus."
Cernunnus replies, "I am a Gaulish (home-born) slave."

"ego sum verna Gallicus," **respondet** Cernunnus.
"I am a Gaulish (home-born) slave," replies Cernunnus.

In Latin, verbs of saying or replying may come *before* their subject, as they sometimes do in English.

2 In the story **15 prope Palātium I**, find and copy out all the verbs of saying and replying. In each case, does the subject come *before* or *after* the verb?

Claudius was the grandnephew of the Emperor Augustus. Claudius was born in Gaul (France), in the city of **Lugdūnum** (Lyon), where his father, the general Germanicus, was posted. Throughout his life, Claudius showed a special affection for Gaul.

Later, when Claudius became Emperor (A.D. 41), he had a better harbor built near Ostia, on the right branch of the Tiber. This greatly improved sea trade between Italy, Gaul, and Hispania.

16 prope Palātium II

Celtillus fīlium audit et ē plaustrō dēscendit. pater fīlium valdē verberat. Rubrius ad lectīcam appropinquat et veniam petit. ecce! in lectīcā est amīcus, Tiberius Claudius. Claudius est iuvenis nōbilis. Claudius in Palātiō habitat. Rubrius est attonitus et veniam iterum petit.

Claudius vernam Cernunnum spectat. "ego quoque sum Gallus," inquit Claudius et rīdet. Cernunnus audit et quoque rīdet. Claudius Rubrium interrogat. Rubrius rem dē servō et dē amphorā nārrat.

"turba in portū Ōstiēnsī est magna," assentit Claudius.

"et portus est parvus," inquit Rubrius.

"vīsitā mē in Palātiō, Rubrī amīce! et tū vīsitā mē, galle Gallice! vīsitāte mē in Palātiō, vōs omnēs!" exclāmat Claudius. "valēte!"

"valē, mī domine Claudī!" respondet Rubrius. Claudius deinde in lectīcā ad Palātium prōcēdit.

"Claudius apud imperātōrem Augustum habitat," inquit Rubrius. "Claudius, ut Caesar Augustus, est vir sapiēns et benevolus."

"et Claudius est amīcus tuus," dīcit sibi Celtillus. Rubrius dēnique cum familiā ad mercātum equitat.

MEANINGS

fīlium	*son*
audit	*hears*
ē plaustrō	*out of the wagon*
dēscendit	*gets down*
valdē	*very much*
verberat	*whips*
lectīcam	*lectica*
appropinquat	*approaches*
veniam petit	*asks for forgiveness*
ecce!	*look!*
in lectīcā	*in a lectica*
amīcus	*friend*
Tiberius Claudius	*Tiberius Claudius, usually simply called Claudius*
iuvenis	*young man*
nōbilis	*noble, aristocratic*
in Palātiō	*on the Palatine hill*
habitat	*lives*
attonitus	*surprised*
iterum	*again*
vernam	*slave (born in master's house)*
ego	*I*
sum	*am*
Gallus	*a Gaul*
inquit	*says*
interrogat	*questions*
rem...nārrat	*tells the story*
dē servō	*about the slave*
dē amphorā	*about the storage jar*
turba	*crowd*
in portū Ōstiēnsī	*in the port of Ostia*
magna	*big*

MEANINGS

assentit	*agrees*
portus	*port*
parvus	*small*
vīsitā!	*visit! (singular)*
mē	*me*
Rubrī!	*Rubrius!*
amīce!	*friend!*
tū	*you (singular)*
galle!	*rooster!*
Gallice!	*Gallic!, Gaulish!*
vīsitāte!	*visit! (plural)*
vōs	*you (plural)*
omnēs	*all*
exclāmat	*exclaims*
valēte!	*goodbye! (plural)*
valē!	*goodbye! (singular)*
mī domine Claudī!	*my lord Claudius!*
respondet	*answers, replies*
deinde	*next, then*
Palātium	*Palatine hill*
prōcēdit	*advances, proceeds*
apud imperātōrem Augustum	*at the house of the Emperor Augustus*
ut Caesar Augustus	*like Caesar Augustus*
vir	*man*
sapiēns	*wise*
benevolus	*kind*
tuus	*your (singular)*
dīcit sibi	*says to himself*
dēnique	*finally*
cum familiā	*with his family*
mercātum	*market*
equitat	*rides (a horse)*

Among the Roman imports from Gaul (and Britain) were hunting dogs which were similar in appearance to the modern breeds of hound. Another popular import from Britain and, later, Hispania, was tin. From the coastal towns of southern Spain came the much-loved salted fish sauce called **garum**, a condiment similar to the modern steak sauces bottled as Worcestershire or A-1 Sauce.

17 emptiō rāra

Rubrius ad portum Ōstiēnsem postrīdiē equitat. Lūcius quoque ad portum Ōstiēnsem equitat. Celtillus plaustrum agit, sed nunc Cernunnus in plaustrō iūxtā patrem sedet. turba prope portum est magna, et portus est parvus. Rubrius in nāvem cōnscendit.

"salvē, mercātor," inquit Rubrius. mercātor Rubrium salūtat. Rubrius magnam amphoram videt. amphora garum Hispānicum continet. Rubrius multās massās videt. massae stanneae sunt ex Britanniā.

"ōhe!" exclāmat Cernunnus. "ecce canis magnus!"

"canis ex Galliā Belgicā venit," explicat mercātor; "canis est vēnāticus."

Cernunnus canem Gallicum dēmulcet. canis caudam laetē vibrat.

"eme canem vēnāticum, pater," clāmat Lūcius. pater annuit, et Lūcius lōrum circum collum affīgit.

"nōmen tuum est Herculēs," inquit Lūcius.

MEANINGS

emptiō	*a purchase*
rāra	*rare*
portum	*port*
Ōstiēnsem	*of Ostia*
postrīdiē	*on the next day*
plaustrum	*wagon*
nunc	*now*
in plaustrō	*in the wagon*
iūxtā	*next to, beside*
patrem	*father*
turba	*crowd*
prope portum	*near the port*
magna	*big*
parvus	*small*
salvē!	*hello!*
mercātor	*merchant*
salūtat	*greets*
magnam	*big*
amphoram	*storage jar, amphora*
garum	*(fish-based) sauce*
Hispānicum	*Hispanic*
continet	*contains*
multās	*many*

MEANINGS

massās	*blocks of metal, ingots*
stanneae	*made of tin*
ex Britanniā	*out of Britain*
sunt	*are*
ōhe!	*ho there!*
exclāmat	*exclaims*
canis	*dog*
magnus	*big*
ex Galliā Belgicā	*out of Belgian Gaul*
venit	*comes*
explicat	*explains*
vēnāticus	*for hunting*
Gallicum	*Gallic, Gaulish*
dēmulcet	*strokes, pets*
caudam	*tail*
laetē	*happily*
vibrat	*waves, wags*
eme!	*buy!*
annuit	*nods toward, agrees*
lōrum	*(leather) collar*
circum collum	*around his neck*
affīgit	*fastens*
nōmen	*a name, the name*
tuum	*your (singular)*
Herculēs	*Hercules*

ACTIVITIES

1 Copy out the following French words onto a piece of paper. French is a modern form of Latin still spoken in France, Québec, Haiti, and other areas of the world:

1 ami	10 mère
2 boire	11 père
3 chien	12 peste
4 clameur	13 pugnace
5 duc	14 scribe
6 exclamation	15 spectre
7 glaive	16 stationner
8 enfant	17 temple
9 jeune	18 voir

2 Find the Latin parent word for each of these French words either in the stories you have read, or in the **Complete Word Meanings** at the back of this book (pp. 70–5). Write down the parent word after each French word.

3 Finally, have an intelligent guess at the meaning of each French word and write it out after its Latin parent word. Check yourself by looking up each word in a French–English dictionary, or by asking your teacher.

18 alter Herculēs

Gāius in hortō lūdit. canis in hortō quoque lūdit. Cernunnus hortum intrat.

"canis est Herculēs alter," exclāmat Cernunnus.

"alter Herculēs est canis," inquit Gāius. Cernunnus fūstem iacit, et Herculēs fūstem ad Cernunnum reportat.

"furcifer!" exclāmat Gāius; "fūstis est gladius meus." Gāius Cernunnum pulsat. dēnique Cernunnus fūstem trādit.

Herculēs ad triclīnium appropinquat. mēnsa in triclīniō stat. cēna est in mēnsā. Herculēs cēnam videt et cōnsūmit. Iūnia ad triclīnium appropinquat et mēnsam spectat.

Specla intrat.

"ubi est cēna?" rogat Iūnia.

"cēna est in mēnsā," inquit Specla.

"cēna in mēnsā nōn est," respondet Iūnia.

nūtrīx Herculem spectat. "mehercle, cēna est in Hercule!" exclāmat Specla.

MEANINGS

alter	*another, a second*
Herculēs	*Hercules*
in hortō	*in the garden*
lūdit	*is playing*
hortum	*garden*
exclāmat	*exclaims*
fūstem	*stick*
iacit	*throws*
reportat	*carries back*
furcifer!	*scoundrel!*
fūstis	*stick*
gladius	*sword*
meus	*my*
pulsat	*hits*
dēnique	*finally*
trādit	*hands over*
triclīnium	*dining room*
appropinquat	*approaches, comes near*
mēnsa	*table*
in triclīniō	*in the dining room*
cēna	*dinner*
in mēnsā	*on the table*
cōnsūmit	*devours, eats*
ubi?	*where?*
rogat	*asks*
mehercle!	*by Hercules!*
in Hercule!	*in Hercules*

PATTERNS

1 The following words always look the same wherever they appear in a Latin sentence:

1 deinde	6 leviter
2 hodiē	7 mox
3 intentē	8 nōn
4 iterum	9 quoque
5 lentē	10 sūrsum deorsum

Words like those above are called *adverbs*. Adverbs usually answer the questions: how? when? where? or why? In Latin, adverbs are usually, though not always, placed before the verb.

2 Write out the English meaning for each of the words above. Compare the forms of the Latin adverbs with the forms of the English adverbs. Is there as much variety in English? What is the most common ending for English adverbs?

Specla tells Lucilia a story about Hercules, the legendary, wandering Greco-Roman hero who once visited Hispania (Portugal and Spain), where she was born.

Hercules walked westward across northern Africa and crossed to Europe at the Rock of Gibraltar. He walked to Gades and crossed to Red Island in a magical cup provided by the Sun god. Sun used this same cup to transport his shining chariot and team of horses each evening from the western side of earth back around the ocean stream to his eastern palace. There, the next morning, he began the new day's sky journey and brought light once again to the world.

It was called Red Island because it lay where Sun glowed red as he drove his chariot down toward the horizon every evening. Red Island was inhabited by a brutal three-headed monster called Geryon. The monster kept a superior herd of cattle that was guarded by a two-headed dog called Orthus.

Red Island was near the ancient Roman city of Gades. Gades was founded by the Phoenician seapeople in about 1100 B.C. They called it **Gadir**, or "Fortress." Its modern name is Cádiz, and it lies on the west coast of what is now the Spanish province of Andalusia. It was from Cádiz, in the sixteenth century A.D., that the Spanish galleons set out for the New World colonies to collect silver.

During Hercules' adventure, he set up Pillars to mark the western boundary of the Mediterranean Sea at the Straits of Gibraltar. Perhaps the legendary Pillars of Hercules were really the twin mountains at Gibraltar and at Ceuta, on the African side of the Straits. The idea of Pillars, however, arose from memories of the temple of **Herculēs Gaditānus** near Gades. (Its ruins still stand today on the tiny island of Sancti Petri.) There, in the temple's courtyard, stood two great columns of gold and silver, the original Pillars of Hercules.

The Pillars, or free-standing columns with a ribbon winding through them, were adapted as a coinage symbol by King Philip V of Spain (ruled A.D. 1700–46). This coinage symbol was copied by the United States government for its first silver dollars, minted in A.D. 1794 from the Spanish silver coins which had been the main currency of the American colonies. This symbol is still used in the United States and Canada as their dollar sign ($). Thus Hercules left his mark even farther west than the ancient Romans would ever have dreamed.

19 prior Herculēs

Specla fābulam Hispānicam nārrat. Lūcīlia fābulam audit:

Herculēs per Africam ad Hispāniam ambulat. in Hispāniā, Herculēs ad Gādēs ambulat. Sōl ferōciter fulget. Herculēs est caldus et valdē īrātus. Herculēs sagittam in Sōlem intendit, sed Sōl rīdet et pōculum aureum (nāvem rāram!) ad Herculem mittit. Herculēs pōculum aureum ad īnsulam occidentālem nāvigat. in īnsulā occidentālī, Herculēs bicipitem canem Orthum interficit, deinde tricipitem dominum Gēryōnem interficit. Herculēs deinde bovēs omnēs in pōculum pōnit, et cum bovibus ad Gādēs nāvigat. ā Gādibus, Herculēs bovēs trāns Hispāniam et deinde trāns Galliam agit ad Ītaliam.

MEANINGS

prior	*prior, the first*
fābulam	*story*
Hispānicam	*Hispanic*
nārrat	*tells*
audit	*hears, listens to*
per Africam	*through Africa*
Hispāniam	*Hispania*
in Hispāniā	*in Hispania*
Gādēs	*Gades (Cádiz)*
Sōl	*Sun*
ferōciter	*fiercely*
fulget	*shines*
caldus	*hot*
valdē	*very*
sagittam	*arrow*
in Sōlem	*at Sun*
intendit	*takes aim*
pōculum	*cup*
aureum	*made of gold, golden*
nāvem	*ship*
rāram	*rare*
mittit	*sends*
īnsulam	*island*
occidentālem	*western*
nāvigat	*sails*
in īnsulā occidentālī	*on the western island*
bicipitem	*two-headed*
canem	*dog*
Orthum	*Orthus*
interficit	*kills*
deinde	*next, then*
tricipitem	*three-headed*
dominum	*owner*
Gēryōnem	*Geryon*
bovēs	*cattle*
omnēs	*all*
in pōculum	*in the cup*
pōnit	*puts*
cum bovibus	*with the cattle*
ā Gādibus	*from Gades*
trāns	*across*
Ītaliam	*Italy*

ACTIVITIES

1 Copy out the following Spanish words onto a piece of paper. Spanish is a modern form of Latin still spoken in Spain, Latin America, and in some areas of the United States:

1 ambulancia	12 gemelo
2 amigo	13 huerto
3 árbol	14 isla
4 bueno	15 madre
5 cena	16 magno
6 clamar	17 muerto
7 correr	18 nuevo
8 decir	19 padre
9 escribir	20 principe
10 fuera	21 saltar
11 gallo	22 tener

2 Find the Latin parent word for each of these Spanish words either in the stories you have read, or in the **Complete Word Meanings** at the back of this book (pp. 70–5). Write down the parent word after each Spanish word.

3 Finally, have an intelligent guess at the meaning of each Spanish word and write it out after its Latin parent word. Check yourself by looking up each word in a Spanish–English dictionary, or by asking your teacher.

PATTERNS

1 Study the following sentences:

Gallus **exit**.   cūr Gallus **exit**?
The Gaul gets out.   *Why does the Gaul get out?*

exī, Galle! clāmat Aegyptius.
"Get out, Gaul!" shouts the Egyptian.

furcifer **festīnat**.   cūr furcifer **festīnat**?
The scoundrel hurries.   *Why does the scoundrel hurry?*

festīnā, furcifer! exclāmat magister.
"Hurry, scoundrel!" exclaims the captain.

Forms of the verb like **exī** and **festīnā** are *commands* ("Get out!" and "Hurry!"). They are often marked in this book, though not in all books, with an exclamation point (!). Commands are forms of the *imperative* mood.

Commands are different from statements, e.g. **exit**, or "s/he gets out" and **festīnat**, or "s/he hurries", or questions, e.g. **cūr exit?** or "Why is s/he getting out?" Statements and questions are forms of the *indicative* mood.

2 Forms of the noun like **Galle!** and **furcifer!** ("Gaul!" and "Scoundrel!") are names used to call someone. When we use names like this, we are using a form called the *vocative* case.

3 Distinguish the vocative case from the subjects, e.g. **Gallus** and **furcifer**, of a statement or a question. Notice the difference between the forms of the noun in the following sentences:

Galle, festīnā!	**Gallus** festīnat.
Gaul, hurry!	*The Gaul is hurrying.*
furcifer, exī!	**furcifer** exit?
Scoundrel, get out!	*Is the scoundrel getting out?*

4 Label the subjects of statements as the *nominative* case. The forms of the words themselves, e.g. nominative **furcifer** and vocative **furcifer**, may be spelled alike.

5 Distinguish the subjects, e.g. **Gallus** and **furcifer**, from the direct objects, e.g. **Gallum** and **furciferum**. Label the direct objects of statements as the *accusative* case. Notice the difference between the forms of the noun in the following sentences:

Gallus festīnat.	Claudius **Gallum** spectat.
The Gaul *is hurrying.*	*Claudius looks at **the Gaul**.*
furcifer exit.	Cernunnus **furciferum** pulsat.
The scoundrel *is getting out.*	*Cernunnus hits **the scoundrel**.*

6 Use the *accusative* case for direct objects. The ending **-m** usually marks an accusative singular form of noun.

nominative	*vocative*	*accusative*
SINGULAR		
fīlia	**fīlia!**	**fīliam**
Gallus	**Galle!**	**Gallum**
Rubrius	**Rubrī!**	**Rubrium**
furcifer	**furcifer!**	**furciferum**

ACTIVITIES

1 On a piece of paper, label three columns (1) *nominative*,
(2) *vocative*, and (3) *accusative*. Then write each of the noun forms
below in the appropriate column:

canis, servum, Rubrī!, Tiberium, amīce, Iūnia, Gallus, māter!,
māter, servus, canis!, serve!, mātrem, Tiberī!, amīcum, Tiberius,
Iūniam, canem, Rubrius, amīcus, Iūnia!, Gallum, Galle!, Rubrium.

2 On a piece of paper, label two columns (1) *imperative* (command),
and (2) *indicative* (statement). Then write each of the forms below
in the appropriate column:

pulsat, salūtā!, cōnscendit, cōnscende!, dormī!, clāmat, venī!,
dormit, salūtat, affīgit, affīge!, pulsā!, venit, clāmā!

3 The statement **salvet** means "s/he is in good health." What does the
command **salvē!** ("Hello!") basically mean? The statement **valet**
means "s/he is strong." What does the command **valē!**
("Goodbye!") basically mean?

Hercules, an ancient cowboy of sorts, slowly drove his cattle across
Spain to southern Gaul. There, near where Marseille would later be
founded, he was attacked by fierce tribespeople called the Ligurians,
who envied him his fine cattle. Hercules was outnumbered and was
nearly killed. But his father Jupiter rained stones down on the
Ligurians. According to legend, these stones still litter the plains west
of modern Marseille.

Eventually, Hercules and the cattle arrived at the site where Rome
would later rise. Hercules camped on the Aventine hill, one of the
seven hills on which Rome would later be built. A merciless beast
called Cacus lived on this hill.

20 Cācus

Herculēs est valdē fessus. Herculēs dēnique in colle Aventīnō dormit.
Cācus spēluncam vīcīnam habitat. Cācus est bēstia ingēns. Cācus ē
spēluncā venit et bovēs in spēluncam retrōrsum trahit. Herculēs posteā
surgit et bovēs nōn videt. Herculēs bovēs ubīque petit. subitō Herculēs
mūgītum audit. euge! Herculēs spēluncam intrat.

"furcifer!" exclāmat Herculēs, et Cācum festīnanter interficit.

MEANINGS

Cācus	*Cacus*
fessus	*tired*
in colle Aventīnō	*on the Aventine hill*
spēluncam	*cave*
vīcīnam	*neighboring*
habitat	*lives in*
bēstia	*beast*
ingēns	*huge*
ē spēluncā	*out of his cave*
venit	*comes*
in spēluncam	*into his cave*
retrōrsum	*backwards (by the tail)*
trahit	*drags*
posteā	*afterwards*
surgit	*gets up*
ubīque	*everywhere*
petit	*seeks, looks for*
subitō	*suddenly*
mūgītum	*the bellowing*
euge!	*hurrah!*

Key Words

1

nouns (subjects)	*adjectives*	*adverbs*	*nouns (direct objects)*	*verbs*
amphora	magna	iterum	amphoram	ambulat
dominus	laetus	festīnanter	dominum	cōnscendit
domus	magnus		domum	dīcit
fābula			fābulam	petit
fūstis			fūstem	pōnit
nāvis			nāvem	respondet
servus			servum	tenet
turba			turbam	vertit
				videt

2 Derivatives: amble, amphoric, component, convert, dictionary, domestic, dominant, fabulous, Leticia, magnify, navy, response, service, tenant, trouble, view.

CHAPTER IV clādēs Germānica

A.D. 9 was a dark year for the Emperor Augustus. His dream of expanding the Roman Empire deep into Germany collapsed. In a surprise attack, the army of the German chieftain Arminius (Hermann, in modern German) almost totally destroyed three legions on parade (some 15,000 unsuspecting soldiers). These legions were commanded by Augustus' deputy, Varus. The soldiers were slaughtered in the Teutoburg Forest, which lay in the modern German provinces of North Rhineland-Westphalia and Lower Saxony.

21 Model Sentences

ancilla historiam audit et tremit.
ancillae historiam audiunt et tremunt.
mīlēs pugnat. mīlitēs pugnant.
mīlēs iacet mortuus. mīlitēs iacent mortuī.
   "vae!" clāmat pater. "vae!" clāmant patrēs.
   "vae!" clāmat māter, "fīlius meus est mortuus."
   "vae!" clāmant mātrēs, "fīliī nostrī sunt mortuī."
servus historiam audit et est laetus. servī historiam audiunt et sunt laetī.

MEANINGS

clādēs	*disaster*
Germānica	*in Germany, German*
ancilla	*slave woman*
historiam	*(historical) account, story*
tremit	*trembles*
ancillae	*slave women*
audiunt	*(they) hear*
tremunt	*(they) tremble*
mīlēs	*soldier*
mīlitēs	*soldiers*
pugnant	*(they) fight*
iacet	*lies*
mortuus	*dead (singular)*
iacent	*(they) lie*
mortuī	*dead (plural)*
vae!	*woe!*
clāmant	*(they) shout*
patrēs	*fathers*
fīlius	*son*
meus	*my*
mātrēs	*mothers*
fīliī	*sons*
nostrī	*our*
sunt	*are*
laetus	*happy*
servi	*slaves*
laetī	*happy (plural)*

22 nūntius advenit

Rubrius in ātriō sedet. vīcīnus iānuam pulsat. Rubrius vīcīnum salutat.

"vae!" exclāmat vīcīnus. "fīlius meus est mortuus." aliī vīcīnī iānuam pulsant.

"ēheu!" clāmant vīcīnī. "trēs legiōnēs in Germāniā sunt victae. omnēs mīlitēs sunt mortuī. Publius Quīntilius Vārus nōn est lēgātus. Vārus est asinus."

"vae!" clāmat Rubrius. "frāter meus in Germāniā iacet mortuus." "vae!" clāmat Iūnia. "frāter meus in Germāniā iacet mortuus." Iūnia valdē lacrimat. Cernunnus rīdet. "Rōmānī sunt victī," dīcit sibi Cernunnus.

MEANINGS

nūntius	*a messenger*
advenit	*arrives*
in ātriō	*in the atrium*
vīcīnus	*neighbor*
iānuam	*door*
pulsat	*hits, knocks on*
vīcīnum	*neighbor*
meus	*my*
aliī	*other (plural)*
vīcīnī	*neighbors*
pulsant	*(they) hit, knock on*
ēheu!	*oh dear!*
clāmant	*(they) shout*
trēs	*three*
legiōnēs	*legions*
in Germāniā	*in Germany*
victae	*beaten*
omnēs	*all*
mīlitēs	*soldiers*
mortuī	*dead (plural)*
Publius Quīntilius Vārus	*Varus*
lēgātus	*general*
asinus	*an ass*
frāter	*brother*
iacet	*lies*
valdē	*very much*
lacrimat	*cries*
Rōmānī	*the Romans*
victī	*beaten*
dīcit sibi	*says to himself*

23 fuga ē proeliō

multī mīlitēs in fossā iacent mortuī. duo mīlitēs in fossā stant
vulnerātī. mīlitēs sunt frīgidī. pluit.

Marcus: vae! Arminius est perfidus.

Sextus: vae! Vārus est stultus.

Marcus: Arminius pācem falsam petit et exercitum Rōmānum
oppugnat.

Sextus: Rōmānī dēcurrunt et Arminius exercitum Rōmānum
oppugnat.

Marcus: vae! nunc multī Rōmānī sunt mortuī.

Marcus et Sextus Augustam Trēverōrum fugiunt.

MEANINGS

fuga	*escape*
ē proeliō	*out of the battle*
multī	*many*
in fossā	*in a ditch*
iacent	*(they) lie*
duo	*two*
stant	*(they) stand, are standing*
vulnerātī	*wounded (plural)*
frīgidī	*cold (plural)*
pluit	*it is raining*
Marcus	*Marcus*
Arminius	*Arminius*
perfidus	*treacherous*
Sextus	*Sextus*
stultus	*stupid*
pācem	*peace*
falsam	*false*
petit	*seeks, asks for*
exercitum	*army*
Rōmānum	*Roman*
oppugnat	*attacks*
Rōmānī	*Romans, the Romans*
dēcurrunt	*are on parade*
exercitum	*army*
oppugnat	*attacks*
Augustam Trēverōrum	*to Augusta Treverorum (Trier)*
fugiunt	*(they) escape*

PATTERNS

1 Study the following sentences:

vīcīnus iānuam **pulsat**.
The neighbor is knocking on the door.

vīcīnī iānuam **pulsant**.
The neighbors are knocking on the door.

vīcīnus is the singular form of the noun when it is the subject of a statement (neighbor). It changes to the plural form **vīcīnī** when the subject is more than one person (neighbors).

2 On a piece of paper, label two columns (1) *nominative singular*, and (2) *nominative plural.* Then write each of the noun forms below in the appropriate column:

Rōmānus, māter, Germānus, nūtrīx, vernae, mātrēs, Germānī, verna, Rōmānī, nūtrīcēs.

3 Study the following sentences:

mīles **est mortuus**.   mīlitēs **sunt mortuī**.
The soldier is dead.   *The soldiers are dead.*

Germānus pācem falsam **petit**.   **Germānī** pācem falsam **petunt**.
The German asks for a false peace.   *The Germans ask for a false peace.*

The plural forms of verb, e.g. **petu***nt*, or "(they) ask for," with plural subjects of statements or questions have a form different from the singular, e.g. **peti***t*, or "asks for."

4 On a piece of paper, label two columns (1) *singular verb*, and (2) *plural verb.* Then write each of the verb forms below in the appropriate column.

iacent, est, oppugnat, stant, clāmat, dormiunt, sunt, tremit, lūdit, iacet, tremunt, dormit, oppugnant, clāmant, stat, lūdunt.

5 Carefully distinguish from the forms above the plural vocative forms of the noun and the plural imperative (command) forms of the verb. The vocative form is usually set off by commas.

vīcīne, pulsā iānuam!   **vīcīnī, pulsāte** iānuam!
Neighbor, knock on the door!   *Neighbors, knock on the door!*

▣ in silvā Germānicā

Marcus et Sextus per silvam fugiunt. multae arborēs in silvā sunt. barbarus in arbore latet. mīles est Germānicus. mīles Germānicus gladium nōn tenet, sed Sextus gladium tenet. Marcus scūtum portat. lūna est plēna et gladius fulget.

subito mīles Germānicus in Sextum ex arbore incidit. barbarus Sextum strangulat. Marcus scūtum dēicit et arborem festīnanter cōnscendit. nunc Marcus in arbore latet. barbarus Marcum quaerit, sed Marcum nōn videt. barbarus dēnique domum currit.

MEANINGS

in silvā Germānicā	*in the German forest*
per silvam	*through the forest*
fugiunt	*(they) escape*
multae	*many*
arborēs	*trees*
in silvā	*in the forest*
barbarus	*the, a barbarian*
in arbore	*in the tree*
latet	*lies hidden*
Germānicus	*of Germany, German, a German*
scūtum	*shield*
portat	*is carrying*
lūna	*moon*
plēna	*full*
fulget	*shines*
in Sextum	*on Sextus*
ex arbore	*out of the tree*
incidit	*falls*
Sextum	*Sextus*
strangulat	*strangles*
dēicit	*throws down*
arborem	*tree*
festīnanter	*quickly*
Marcum	*Marcus*
quaerit	*looks for*
domum	*home(wards)*
currit	*runs*

ACTIVITY

Translate all the words below, including the words in brackets. Then look at each phrase and choose one of the words in brackets to make a sensible sentence. Translate the completed sentence.

1 Rōmānī (tremit, tremunt).
2 Arminius pācem falsam (petunt, petit).
3 lēgātus Arminium nōn (suspiciunt, suspicit).
4 Rōmānī (dēcurrit, dēcurrunt).
5 Germānī (oppugnant, oppugnat).
6 multī mīlitēs (iacet, iacent) mortuī.
7 Vārus (iacent, iacet) mortuus.
8 Augustus (lacrimant, lacrimat).

Marcus, the sole survivor of the disaster in the Teutoburg Forest, escapes to **Augusta Trēverōrum** (modern Trier).

Trier is modern Germany's oldest town. It was first established in 16 B.C. by Augustus on the navigable Mosel river, on the site of a settlement of the Gaulish tribespeople called the **Trēverī**. Caesar, Augustus' adopted father, had conquered the Treveri earlier. Augusta Treverorum had a regular street grid and, at first, only wooden buildings. You can still see the ruins of Roman baths and an amphitheater, which dates from periods later than this story.

25 in Augustā Trēverōrum

multī mīlitēs sunt in oppidō Augustā Trēverōrum. mīlitēs sunt custōdēs. Marcus oppidum intrat. Marcus, ut Germānus, pellem gerit. custōdēs Marcum dērīdent et comprehendunt. custōdēs deinde Marcum ad prōcūrātōrem dūcunt.

prōcūrātor pellem videt, sed nōn dērīdet. Marcus linguam Latīnam dīcit! prōcūrātor ergō Marcum ad thermās dūcit. ibi Marcus rem nārrat:

> Rōmānī et Germānī pugnant. Arminius, prīnceps Germānicus, pācem falsam petit. Vārus, lēgātus Rōmānus, nihil suspicit. mīlitēs Rōmānī dēcurrunt. subitō Germānī in exercitum Rōmānum incidunt. Rōmānī fortiter pugnant, sed paene omnēs nunc iacent mortuī. barbarī sunt victōrēs.

prōcūrātor est valdē maestus.

MEANINGS

in Augustā Trēverōrum	*in Augusta Treverorum (Trier)*
multī	*many*
in oppidō Augustā Trēverōrum	*in the town (of) Augusta Treverorum*
custōdēs	*guards*
oppidum	*town*
ut Germānus	*like a German*
pellem	*skin*
gerit	*is wearing*
dērīdent	*(they) make fun of*
comprehendunt	*(they) arrest*
prōcūrātōrem	*Emperor's finance agent, procurator*
dūcunt	*(they) lead*
linguam Latīnam	*Latin language*
dīcit	*says, speaks*
ergō	*therefore*
thermās	*baths*
dūcit	*leads*
ibi	*there*
rem nārrat	*tells his story*
prīnceps	*chieftain*
pācem	*peace*
falsam	*false*
petit	*seeks, looks for*
lēgātus	*general*
Rōmānus	*Roman*
nihil	*nothing*
suspicit	*suspects*
dēcurrunt	*are on parade*
in exercitum Rōmānum	*on the Roman army*
incidunt	*(they) fall*
fortiter	*bravely*
paene	*almost*
barbarī	*the barbarians*
victōrēs	*the winners*
valdē	*very*
maestus	*sad*

ACTIVITIES

1 Copy out the following German words onto a piece of paper. Like English, German is a language which did not originally come from Latin. But because of military and economic contacts between the Roman and German peoples, modern German contains some words of Latin derivation. For example:

1 Ambulanz	9 Legat
2 Amphitheater	10 Legion
3 Barbarei	11 Masse
4 Karte	12 Pädagoge
5 Kustos	13 Pfalz
6 Flamme	14 römisch
7 Imperialismus	15 servieren
8 Kaiser	16 Wein

2 Find the Latin parent word for each of these German words either in the stories you have read or in the **Complete Word Meanings** at the back of this book (pp. 70–5). Write the parent word out after each German word.

3 Finally, make an intelligent guess at the meaning of each German word and write it out after its Latin parent word. Check yourself by looking up each word in a German–English dictionary or by asking your teacher.

The **Capitōlium** was the most sacred of the seven hills of Rome. There the Romans built the great temple of the three high gods: Jupiter Optimus Maximus ("Jupiter the best and greatest"), his wife Juno, and his daughter Minerva. Augustus renovated the temple twice in the years before this story. It was here that Augustus met with the people at times of crises like that of the German disaster.

Many Italian towns and some cities, like Roman Byzantium and Jerusalem under the Emperor Hadrian (A.D. 117–38), imitated the city of Rome by building their own "Capitols," or hills with temples. The Roman tradition has survived in Washington, D.C., which has a Capitol Hill, where the Capitol was built to house the Congress of the United States.

26 Rōmae

Rubrius et Iūnia et Lūcius ad templum Capitōlīnum contendunt. Gāius et Cernunnus prōcurrunt. magna turba est in viā. omnēs virī sunt maestī. multae fēminae lacrimant.

Iuppiter Optimus Maximus in templō Capitōlīnō sedet. Augustus prō templō stat. Augustus togam pullam gerit et ōrātiōnem habet:

> prīnceps Arminius est valdē perfidus. Arminius pācem falsam petit et exercitum Rōmānum oppugnat. tres legiōnēs nunc dēsunt. multī mīlitēs Rōmānī nunc in Germāniā iacent mortuī. Vāre, legiōnēs redde!

Augustus publicē lacrimat. multī spectātōrēs – virī et fēminae, puerī et puellae – quoque lacrimant. Cernunnus tamen nōn lacrimat.

MEANINGS

Rōmae	*in Rome*
templum	*temple*
Capitōlīnum	*the Capitoline hill*
contendunt	*(they) hurry*
prōcurrunt	*(they) run ahead*
in viā	*in the street*
virī	*men*
maestī	*sad (plural)*
multae	*many*
fēminae	*women*
lacrimant	*(they) are crying*
Iuppiter Optimus Maximus	*Jupiter the best and greatest*
in templō Capitōlīnō	*in his temple on the Capitoline hill*
togam pullam	*dark gray toga (mourning garment)*
gerit	*is wearing*
ōrātiōnem habet	*makes a speech*
prīnceps	*chieftain*
valdē	*very*
perfidus	*treacherous*
pācem	*peace*
falsam	*false*
petit	*asks for*
exercitum	*army*
Rōmānum	*Roman (singular)*
oppugnat	*attacks*
trēs	*three*

MEANINGS

legiōnēs	*legions*
dēsunt	*(they) are missing*
Rōmānī	*Roman (plural)*
Vāre!	*Varus!*
redde!	*give back!*
publicē	*publicly*
spectātōrēs	*spectators*
puerī	*boys*
puellae	*girls*
tamen	*however*

ACTIVITY

Translate all the words below, including the words in brackets. Then look at each phrase and choose one of the words in brackets to make a sensible sentence. Translate the completed sentence.

1 (custōdēs, lēgātī) Marcum ad prōcūrātōrem dūcunt.
2 (Marcus, barbarus) linguam Latīnam dīcit.
3 (prōcūrātor, Arminius) est laetus.
4 (custōs, prōcūrātor) Marcum ad thermās dūcit.
5 ibi (servī, prōcūrātor) Marcum cūrant.
6 ibi (Marcus, Germānus) rem nārrat.
7 (prōcūrātor, Arminius) est maestus.

Key Words

1

nouns (plural) subjects	adjectives (plural)	adverbs	nouns (singular) direct objects	verbs (plural)
ancillae	mortuae	nunc	frātrem	audiunt
frātrēs	maestī	fortiter	silvam	dūcunt
silvae	maestae	subitō		lacrimant
				latent
				pugnant
				pulsant
				rīdent

2 Derivatives: audience, deride, duct, fortitude, fraternity, lachrymose, latent, mortuary, pugnacious, pulsate, Silvester.

CHAPTER V salūtātiō

Freeborn Roman men had three names. Their family name was the middle name, not the last name, as in English names. For example, the personal name of **Gāius Iūlius Caesar** was **Gāius** (given to him at the time of his **lūstrātiō**). This Gaius belonged to the Caesarian branch of the larger Julian clan. Freeborn women were often given a single name, the feminine form of their clan's name. For example, Gaius Iulius Caesar and his adopted son Gaius Iulius Caesar Octavianus Augustus both named their daughters **Iūlia** (Julia).

27 Model Sentences

servus:	quis es tū?	alius:	ego sum Titus Rubrius Valēns.
	quid tū agis?		ego negōtium agō. ego sum mercātor.
	quis es tū?		ego sum Lūcius Rubrius Valēns.
	quid tū agis?		ego patrem meum adiuvō.
	quis es tū?		ego sum Gāius Rubrius Valēns. ego in lūdō discō. ego sum discipulus.
	quis es tū?		ego sum Cernunnus.
	quid tū agis?		ego valdē labōrō. ego sum verna.

MEANINGS

salūtātiō	a, the visit
quis?	who?
es	(you) are (singular)
tū	you (singular)
alius	the other (person)
ego	I
sum	am
Titus Rubrius Valēns	Rubrius (full name of)
quid?	what?
agis	you do (singular)
negōtium agō	(I) am in business
Lūcius Rubrius Valēns	Lucius (full name of)
patrem	father
meum	my
adiuvō	(I) help, am helping
Gāius Rubrius Valēns	Gaius (full name of)
in lūdō	in school
discō	(I) learn
discipulus	student
valdē	very much, a lot
labōrō	(I) work
verna	slave (born in master's house)

Rubrius accepts Claudius' invitation to visit him at Augustus' palace on the Palatine hill (see Stories **15** and **16 prope Palātium I** and **II**). The young Claudius is a friendly host. He can't help noticing that Rubrius' sons are named after Augustus' grandsons, Gaius and Lucius. They were adopted by Augustus as full sons and heirs in 17 B.C. Both boys died, however, some 20 years later. Augustus was bitterly disappointed and could only adopt his unpopular stepson Tiberius.

28 domus Augustāna

servus: salvē! quis es tū? cūr venīs?

Rubrius: ego Titus Rubrius Valēns sum. ego dominum Claudium vīsitō. (*servus Rubrium ad Claudium dūcit. Lūcius et puerī quoque veniunt.*)

Claudius: salvēte, omnēs! euge! ego puerum Gallicum videō. quid est nōmen tuum?

Cernunnus:	nōmen meum est Cernunnus.
Claudius:	*(Claudius Lūcium spectat.)* et quid est nōmen tuum?
Lūcius:	Lūcius Rubrius Valēns est nōmen meum.
Claudius:	*(Claudius Gāium spectat.)* et quid est nōmen tuum?
Gāius:	Gāius Rubrius Valēns est nōmen meum.
Claudius:	Gāius. ēheu!
Cernunnus:	cūr tū "ēheu" clāmās?
Claudius:	Gāius et Lūcius, nepōtēs Augustī, sunt mortuī. avus Augustus est maestus. et nunc trēs legiōnēs in Germāniā dēsunt. Augustus per domum ambulat et clāmat, "Vāre, legiōnēs redde!"
	ego tamen forās ambulō. venīte, omnēs! *(exeunt.)*

MEANINGS

domus	*house*	tamen	*however*
Augustāna	*of Augustus*	forās	*outside*
es	*you are (singular)*	ambulō	*I am going to walk*
cūr?	*why?*	venīte!	*come! (plural)*
venīs	*you come (singular)*	exeunt	*they go out*
dominum	*lord*		
vīsitō	*(I) am visiting*		
dūcit	*leads*		
puerī	*boys*		
veniunt	*(they) come*		
salvēte!	*hello! (plural)*		
euge!	*hurrah!*		
puerum	*boy*		
Gallicum	*Gallic, Gaulish*		
videō	*(I) see*		
quid?	*what?*		
nōmen	*name*		
tuum	*your (singular)*		
meum	*my*		
clāmās	*(you) shout (singular)*		
nepōtēs Augustī	*grandsons of Augustus*		
avus	*grandfather*		
maestus	*sad*		
trēs	*three*		
legiōnēs	*legions*		
dēsunt	*(they) are missing*		
per domum	*through the house*		
Vāre!	*Varus!*		
redde!	*give back!*		

PATTERNS

1 Study the following sentences:

"ego **veniō**," inquit Marcus.
"I am coming," says Marcus.

Marce, cūr tū **venīs**?
O Marcus, why are you coming?

cūr Marcus **venit**?
Why is Marcus coming?

Forms of the verb change depending on the subject of the verb.

2 The "I" ending (-ō) is labeled *first person singular.* The "you" (singular) ending (-s) is labeled *second person singular.*
The "she, he, or it" ending *(-t)* is labeled *third person singular.*
The "they" ending (-**nt**) is labeled *third person plural.*

3 Study the following chart:

first person singular	*second person singular*	*third person singular*	*third person plural*
portō	**portās**	**portat**	**porta**nt
I carry	*you carry*	*s/he, it carries*	*they carry*
habeō	**habēs**	**habet**	**habe**nt
I have	*you have*	*s/he, it has*	*they have*
vertō	**vertis**	**vertit**	**vertu**nt
I turn	*you turn*	*s/he, it turns*	*they turn*
capiō	**capis**	**capit**	**capiu**nt
I take	*you take*	*s/he, it takes*	*they take*
audiō	**audīs**	**audit**	**audiu**nt
I hear	*you hear*	*s/he, it hears*	*they hear*
sum	**es**	**est**	**su**nt
I am	*you are*	*s/he, it is*	*they are*

4 On a piece of paper, label four columns (1) *first person singular verb*, (2) *second person singular verb*, (3) *third person singular verb*, and (4) *third person plural verb*. Then write each of the verb forms below in the appropriate column:

adiuvō, es, ambulās, discō, sedent, contendis, habeō, dormiō, ambulant, ambulat, habēs, dormīs, sunt, adiuvat, discit, contendō, sedēs, habent, dormit, contendit, adiuvās, sum, ambulō, sedeō, habet, discis, dormiunt.

Claudius was physically handicapped: he had difficulty in walking. He also had a speech impediment. Because of this, or perhaps in spite of this, Claudius was unique among members of the imperial family for his interest in books and scrolls. He especially liked reading about the traditions and history of the Roman people. True to his scholarly interests, Claudius entertains the boys in Rubrius' family with a story about the founding of Rome.

29 in colle Palātīnō I

Claudius in colle Palātīnō ambulat, sed iuvenis nōbilis claudicat.
　　"ecce! ca-casa Rōmulī," balbūtit Claudius.
　　"quis est Rōmulus?" rogat Cernunnus.
　　"ego sum fessus," respondet Claudius. "sedēte, puerī! fābulam audīte!" Gāius et Cernunnus humī sedent.

Numitor et Amūlius sunt frātrēs. Numitor et Amūlius oppidum Albam Longam simul regunt. Amūlius tamen frātrem Numitōrem ōdit. Amūlius Numitōrem ex Albā Longā fugat. Amūlius posteā regit sōlus. Numitor ūnam fīliam, Rheam, habet. Rhea est virgō Vestālis. Rhea flammam aeternam in forō cūrat. deus Mars ē caelō ad terram venit, et oppidum Albam Longam vīsitat. Mars virginem pulchram videt. Mars Rheam valdē amat. Rhea posteā geminōs parit. geminī sunt Rōmulus et Remus. Amūlius est īrātus. Amūlius Rheam in carcerem pōnit. duo servī tamen Rōmulum et Remum in canistrum pōnunt. servī deinde canistrum in flūmen Tiberim pōnunt.

MEANINGS

in colle Palātīnō	*on the Palatine hill*
iuvenis	*young man*
nōbilis	*noble, aristocratic*
claudicat	*is lame, limps*
casa Rōmulī	*Romulus' hut*
balbūtit	*stutters*
Rōmulus	*Romulus*
rogat	*asks*
fessus	*tired*
sedēte!	*sit! (plural)*
audīte!	*listen to!*
humī	*on the ground*
Numitor	*Numitor*
Amūlius	*Amulius*
frātrēs	*brothers*
oppidum Albam Longam	*town (of) Alba Longa*
simul	*together*
regunt	*(they) rule*
frātrem	*brother*
ōdit	*hates*
ex Albā Longā	*out of Alba Longa*
fugat	*chases*
posteā	*afterwards*
regit	*rules*
sōlus	*alone*
ūnam	*one*
fīliam	*daughter*
Rheam	*Rhea, the beloved of Mars; mother of the twins Romulus and Remus*
virgō Vestālis	*Vestal Virgin*
flammam aeternam	*eternal flame (the symbolic hearth-fire of the town)*
in forō	*in the forum*
cūrat	*takes care of*
deus	*god*
Mars	*Mars*
ē caelō	*out of heaven*
terram	*earth*
venit	*comes*
vīsitat	*visits*

virginem	*virgin*
pulchram	*beautiful*
valdē	*very much*
amat	*is in love with*
geminōs	*twins*
parit	*gives birth to*
Remus	*Remus*
in carcerem	*into jail*
duo	*two*
in canistrum	*into a basket*
in flūmen Tiberim	*into the Tiber river*

ACTIVITY

Translate all the words below, including the words in brackets. Then look at each phrase and choose one of the words in brackets to make a sensible sentence. Translate the completed sentence.

1 ego Claudium (vīsitat, vīsitō).
2 Lūcius et Gāius Claudium quoque (vīsitat, vīsitant).
3 Claudius, "salvēte!" (dīcis, dīcit).
4 Claudius Gāium (spectō, spectat).
5 Claudius Gāium (rogās, rogat), "tū canem (habet, habēs)?"

Augustus' palace was located in the area where Rome's founder, the legendary Romulus, had built the first humble house in Rome. It was an oval hut with a thatched roof, to commemorate the place where the she-wolf had supposedly suckled Romulus. This "first house" was supposedly preserved and put on display, complete with thatched roof, in Augustus' day.

30 in colle Palātīnō II

Cernunnus:	quid deinde accidit? geminī sunt mortuī?
Gāius:	ego sciō. lupa Rōmulum et Remum invenit.
Cernunnus:	et lupa Rōmulum et Remum interficit?
Gāius:	tū es stultus!
Claudius:	tacēte, ambō! ego fābulam nārrō. lupa Rōmulum et Remum cūrat. pāstor deinde Rōmulum et Remum cūrat. sīc geminī adolēscunt.
Gāius:	cūr Rōmulus casam in colle Palātīnō habet?
Claudius:	geminī Amūlium dēnique interficiunt, et avum Numitōrem ad oppidum Albam Longam redūcunt. geminī dēnique urbem novam condunt.
Cernunnus:	ubi est urbs nova?
Gāius:	tū es stultus! ego sciō. urbs nova est Rōma.
Claudius:	et ecce! casa Rōmulī.
Cernunnus:	et ubi est casa Remī?
Claudius:	Remus casam nōn habet. Remus est inimīcus.
Cernunnus:	cūr est Remus inimīcus?
Claudius:	Remus Rōmulum dērīdet.
Cernunnus:	et ego Gāium dērīdeō.
Claudius:	puerī! puerī!
Gāius:	multās grātiās. tū fābulam bonam nārrās.

MEANINGS

in colle Palātīnō	*on the Palatine hill*
accidit	*happens*
geminī	*twins*
sciō	*(I) know*
lupa	*she-wolf*
invenit	*finds*
es	*(you) are (singular)*
stultus	*stupid*
tacēte!	*be quiet! (plural)*
ambō	*both*
nārrō	*(I) tell*
cūrat	*takes care of*
pāstor	*shepherd*
sīc	*thus*
adolēscunt	*(they) grow up*
cūr?	*why?*
casam	*hut*
avum	*grandfather*
oppidum Albam Longam	*town (of) Alba Longa*

redūcunt	*(they) lead back*
urbem	*city*
novam	*new*
condunt	*(they) found, establish*
urbs	*city*
nova	*new*
Rōma	*(city of) Rome*
casa Rōmulī	*Romulus' hut*
ubi?	*where?*
casa Remī	*Remus' hut*
inimīcus	*the enemy*
dērīdet	*makes fun of*
et	*too, also*
puerī!	*boys!*
multās	*many*
grātiās	*thanks*
bonam	*good*
nārrās	*you tell*

Key Words

1

nouns (plural) subjects	adjectives (plural)	adverb	nouns (singular) direct objects	verbs (plural)
casae	sōlae	posteā	casam	interficiunt
deī	multī		deum	vīsitant
legiōnēs	multae		legiōnem	
mercātōrēs			mercātōrem	
puellae			puellam	
puerī			puerum	
urbēs			urbem	
vernae			vernam	

2 **Derivatives:** adieu (French), legionnaire, merchandise, multiply, posterior, puerile, solitaire, urbane, vernacular, visitor.

59

CHAPTER VI

Sāturnāliā

Celtillus, Rubrius' adult slave, was captured as a boy in northeastern Gaul during one of Augustus' campaigns there (15–13 B.C.). Augustus' conquest of northeastern Gaul finally brought a Roman peace to the whole of Gaul.

Celtillus was later sold by aides to Augustus, who had captured him, in a Roman slave market. Celtillus belonged to the last generation of Gaulish people who remembered a time when at least part of Gaul was free.

31 Model Sentences

Specla ōlim erat lībera.

Cernunnus ōlim erat īnfāns. Cernunnus nunc est puer.
Specla ōlim erat lībera. Specla nunc est nūtrīx.
Celtillus ōlim erat līber. Celtillus nunc est servus.
Celtillus et Specla ōlim erant aliēnī. Celtillus et Specla nunc sunt servī Rōmānī.
Celtillus puer in Galliā ōlim lūdēbat. subitō Celtillus clāmōrem audīvit.
Celtillus puer mīlitēs Rōmānōs fugiēbat. mīlitēs Rōmānī Celtillum comprehendērunt.
Celtillus et aliī puerī ut servī ad Ītaliam nāvigābant.
custōs Rōmānus Celtillum in nāve ōlim verberāvit.

MEANINGS

Sāturnālia	*the Saturnalia (festival)*
ōlim	*once (in the past)*
erat	*(s/he) was*
puer	*boy*
lībera, f.	*free*
līber, m.	*free*
erant	*(they) were*
aliēnī	*foreigners*
Rōmānī	*in Rome, Roman*
in Galliā	*in Gaul*
lūdēbat	*(he) used to play*
clāmōrem	*a shout*
audīvit	*(he) heard*
fugiēbat	*(he) was running away from*

MEANINGS

comprehendērunt	*(they) arrested*
aliī	*other (plural)*
ut servī	*as slaves*
Ītaliam	*Italy*
nāvigābant	*(they) were sailing*
custōs	*guard*
in nāve	*on the ship*
verberāvit	*whipped*

A reconstruction of the siegeworks at Alesia.

Vercingetorix was chieftain of a Gaulish tribe called the Arverni. Like the German chieftain Arminius some sixty years later, Vercingetorix managed to terrorize the invading Romans, though less successfully than Arminius. At a council of Gaulish leaders, Vercingetorix persuaded them to support his "scorched earth" policy. They themselves would destroy all the Gaulish villages in the line of the Romans' advance. In one day, more than 220 towns of the Bituriges tribe (in the area of modern Bourges) were set on fire. The sight of the smoke made the Romans panic, and thereby steeled the nerve of additional Gaulish tribes to rebel.

At the peak of the Gaulish rebellion, Vercingetorix withdrew his army to the town of Alesia (modern Alise-Ste-Reine, 30 miles northwest of Dijon), the last rallying point of Gaulish nationalism. Caesar and the Roman legions laid siege to the town, and the Gaulish forces were unable to relieve it. Eventually, the desperate elders of Alesia were forced to surrender their town, themselves, and Vercingetorix.

Many centuries later, in the 1860s, the French Emperor Napoleon III had the battle site at Alise-Ste-Reine excavated. The excavators uncovered evidence of the siege lines of both the Gauls and the Romans.

The Dying Gaul.

32 Vercingetorix

Cernunnus et Gāius in hortō lūdēbant. Gāius erat mīles Rōmānus, et Cernunnus erat mīles Gallicus. Gāius Cernunnum pulsāvit. Cernunnus erat maestus, sed nōn lacrimābat.

"Rōmānī semper sunt victōrēs," inquit Cernunnus. subitō Celtillus hortum intrāvit.

"Rōmānī nōn semper erant victōrēs," inquit Celtillus. "Vercingetorix ōlim erat dux Gallicus. Vercingetorix Iūlium Caesarem diu vexābat. dux Gallicus lēgātum Rōmānum diū fraudābat, sed Caesar dēnique superāvit. Vercingetorix et mīlitēs Gallicī in oppidum Alesiam reccidērunt. aliī mīlitēs Gallicī in exercitum Rōmānum incidērunt. mīlitēs Rōmānī post proelium longum erant victōrēs. Vercingetorix in Alesiā manēbat, sed senēs Alesiēnsēs Vercingetorigem ad Caesarem dēnique tradidērunt. Vercingetorix nunc est mortuus, sed tū es vīvus."

Cernunnus, postquam rem audīvit, erat laetus. Gāius tamen erat īrātus.

MEANINGS

Vercingetorix	*Vercingetorix*
in hortō	*in the garden*
lūdēbant	*(they) were playing*
pulsāvit	*(he) hit*
maestus	*sad*
lacrimābat	*was crying*
semper	*always*
victōrēs	*the winners*
hortum	*garden*
intrāvit	*(he) entered*
erant	*(they) were*
dux	*leader*
Iūlium Caesarem	*Iulius (Julius) Caesar*
diū	*for a long time*
vexābat	*(he) kept annoying*
lēgātum	*general*
fraudābat	*(he) cheated*
superāvit	*(he) won*
in oppidum Alesiam	*to the town (of) Alesia*
recciderunt	*(they) fell back, retreated*
aliī	*other (plural)*
in exercitum Rōmānum	*on the Roman army*
inciderunt	*(they) fell*
post proelium longum	*after a long battle*
in Alesiā	*in Alesia*
manēbat	*(he) stayed behind*
senēs	*old men*
Alesiēnsēs	*of Alesia, Alesian*
trādidērunt	*(they) handed over, surrendered*
vīvus	*alive*
postquam	*after*
rem	*the event, the story*
audīvit	*he heard*
laetus	*happy*

PATTERNS

1 Study the following sentences:

Vercingetorix Caesarem **vexat.**
Vercingetorix annoys Caesar.

Vercingetorix Caesarem **vexābat.**
Vercingetorix kept annoying Caesar.

Vercingetorix Caesarem **vexāvit.**
Vercingetorix annoyed Caesar.

Verb forms in the past tenses, e.g. **vexābat** and **vexāvit**, are formed differently from verb forms in the present tense, e.g. **vexat**.

2 Contrast the following pairs of sentences:

senēs Gallōs **verberābant.**
The elders kept whipping Gauls (over a period of time).

senēs Vercingetorigem **verberāvērunt.**
The elders whipped Vercingetorix (once).

The forms of the past tense used to describe continued or repeated action, e.g. **verberābant**, are labeled *imperfect tense*. The forms of the past tense used to describe simple or single action, e.g. **verberāvērunt**, are labeled *perfect tense*.

3 Study the following chart:

PRESENT TENSE		IMPERFECT TENSE		PERFECT TENSE	
singular	*plural*	*singular*	*plural*	*singular*	*plural*
portat	**portant**	**portābat**	**portābant**	**portāvit**	**portāvērunt**
he* carries	*they carry*	*he was carrying*	*they were carrying*	*he carried*	*they carried*
habet	**habent**	**habēbat**	**habēbant**	**habuit**	**habuērunt**
he has	*they have*	*he used to have*	*they used to have*	*he had*	*they had*
vertit	**vertunt**	**vertēbat**	**vertēbant**	**vertit**	**vertērunt**
he turns	*they turn*	*he kept turning*	*they kept turning*	*he turned*	*they turned*
capit	**capiunt**	**capiēbat**	**capiēbant**	**cēpit**	**cēpērunt**
he takes	*they take*	*he was taking*	*they were taking*	*he took*	*they took*
audit	**audiunt**	**audiēbat**	**audiēbant**	**audīvit**	**audīvērunt**
he hears	*they hear*	*he kept hearing*	*they kept hearing*	*he heard*	*they heard*
est	**sunt**	**erat**	**erant**		
he is	*they are*	*he was*	*they were*		

***Note:** All "he" forms may also be, depending on context, "she" or "it."

Notice that the imperfect verb forms may be translated in several ways, depending on the sense demanded by the sentence. For example:

pulsābat s/he, it was hitting, kept hitting, used to hit, would hit
pulsābant they were hitting, kept hitting, used to hit, would hit.

ACTIVITIES

1 On a piece of paper, label three columns (1) *3rd person singular present verb*, (2) *3rd person singular imperfect verb*, and (3) *3rd person singular perfect verb*. Then write each of the verb forms below in the appropriate column:

erat, lūdēbat, vexāvit, lacrimat, verberat, est, nāvigābat, lūdit, nāvigāvit, lūsit, lacrimābat, verberāvit, vexābat, vexat, lacrimāvit, verberābat, nāvigat.

2 Find the forms in the list of Activity 1 above that mean: she played, he used to whip, he sails, it is, he kept annoying.

The days of the **Sāturnālia** came at last (December 17). This festival was celebrated annually in honor of the god Saturn, who was king during the Golden Age when there were no divisions between masters and slaves, or rich and poor. The Saturnalia marked the return of the Golden Age for a few days every year. It was the happiest of all the Roman festivals.

During the days of the Saturnalia, the masters of the house had to do the work, while the slaves rested and enjoyed themselves. The children received small, but amusing gifts. Dinner parties during the Saturnalia were joyful and colorful events. Slaves and other dinner guests were allowed to replace their dull clothes with brightly patterned robes, and even to parade in the streets wearing them. The noise, the good cheer, the unusual clothes, the toys, and especially the general confusion, were like Halloween, Christmas, New Year, and Mardi Gras all rolled into one.

33 Sāturnālia I

Iūnia, quod familia Sāturnālia celebrābat, in culīnā cēnam parābat. servī in triclīniō recumbēbant. Rubrius et Lūcius serviēbant. Cernunnus togam et pilleum gerēbat.

subitō Cernunnus clāmāvit, "Vercingetorix ōlim erat dux Gallicus. Rōmānī perfidī Galliam invāsērunt. Gallī fortiter resistēbant. ēheu! Rōmānī dēnique erant victōrēs. dux Vercingetorix nunc est mortuus.

ego tamen sum alter Vercingetorix! Gallī iterum sunt victōrēs."
Cernunnus sūrsum deorsum saliēbat. Cernunnus iterum et iterum
fūstem vibrābat.

    "tū es stultus," clāmāvit Gāius.

    "et nimis audax," dīxit sibi Celtillus. Celtillus Cernunnum
comprehendit et fortiter verberāvit. Cernunnus ululāvit et Gāius "iō
Sāturnālia!" exclāmāvit.

MEANINGS

Sāturnālia	*the Saturnalia (festival)*
quod	*because*
familia	*the family*
celebrābat	*was celebrating*
in culīnā	*in the kitchen*
parābat	*(she) was preparing*
in triclīniō	*in the dining room*
recumbēbant	*(they) were lying down*
serviēbant	*(they) were waiting on them*
togam	*wool mantle worn (except at the Saturnalia) by citizens, toga*
pilleum	*a felt cap (shaped like half an egg)*
dux	*leader*
perfidī	*treacherous (plural)*
Galliam	*Gaul*
invāsērunt	*(they) invaded*
Gallī	*the Gauls*
fortiter	*fiercely*
resistēbant	*(they) resisted*
alter	*another, a second*
iterum	*again*
fūstem	*stick*
vibrābat	*(he) kept waving*
nimis	*excessively, too*
audax	*daring*
dīxit sibi	*(he) said to himself*
comprehendit	*(he) arrested, grabbed*
ululāvit	*(he) howled*
iō Sāturnālia!	*hurrah, the Saturnalia!*
exclāmāvit	*(he) exclaimed*

ACTIVITY

Make the Latin sentence in each pair match the English one by writing out (on a separate piece of paper) the correct choice of verb in brackets. If you are not sure about the correct choice, look up the chart on p. 64 above or in the **Complete Word Patterns** (inside back cover).

1 Celtillus patrem diū (vexāvit, vexābat).
Celtillus kept annoying his father for a long time.

2 custōdēs Rōmānī Gallōs semper (comprehendērunt, comprehendēbant).
The Roman guards would always arrest Gauls.

3 subitō Celtillus clāmōrem (audiēbat, audīvit).
Suddenly, Celtillus heard a shout.

4 subitō Rōmānī oppidum Gallicum (oppugnābant, oppugnāvērunt).
The Romans attacked the Gaulish town suddenly.

5 Rōmānī dēnique Celtillum (comprehendēbant, comprehendērunt).
Finally, the Romans arrested Celtillus.

During the Saturnalia, Rubrius' family learns that they are moving to **Lugdūnum** (modern Lyon). Lugdunum was the administrative capital of the "Three Gauls." They were the three provinces that Augustus shaped out of the area which he and Caesar had taken over: Belgian Gaul, Lugdunensian Gaul, and Aquitanian Gaul. As Augustus' finance agent, Rubrius is to be in charge of financial collections, taxes, and disbursements. Being a good businessman, he is undoubtedly expected to make a profit for the Emperor.

During the Saturnalia story, we learn that Lucilia, Rubrius' foster daughter (**alumna**), expects to become Lucius' wife. At least, that is the implication of her silent echoing of her mother's words, "ubi ego Rubrium habeō, ibi ego sum laeta." Her words are very like a Roman bride's at her marriage, **ubi tū Gāius, ibi et ego sum Gāia.** These can be expressed in English as, "Wherever you're my Gaius, that's where I, too, am your Gaia." **Gāius** and **Gāia**, like English *Jack* and *Jill*, were very common Latin names.

34 Sāturnālia II

familia, postquam cēnāvit, per viam ambulābat. Rubrius et Lūcius synthesēs gerēbant. magna turba erat in viā. multī puerī et puellae lūdēbant in viā. Iūnia et Lūcīlia simul ambulābant. Lūcīlia īnfantem Rubriam portābat.

"māter," rogāvit Lūcīlia, "cūr ad Galliam iter facimus?"

"nostra domus nova," respondit māter, "est in Galliā. pater tuus nunc est prōcūrātor Augustī."

"māter," inquit Lūcīlia, "Gallī nunc in silvā latent?"

"nōn latent," respondit Iūnia. "Germānī, quod sunt barbarī, in silvā latent. Gallī tamen vīllās in oppidīs nunc habitant."

"Gallia est procul?" rogāvit Lūcīlia.

"Gallia est procul," respondit Iūnia, "sed ubi ego Rubrium habeō, ibi ego sum laeta."

"et ubi ego Lūcium habeō, ibi et ego sum laeta," dīxit sibi Lūcīlia.

MEANINGS

postquam	*after*
cēnāvit	*(it) ate dinner*
per viam	*through the street*
synthesēs	*colored robes*
magna	*a great*
puellae	*girls*
simul	*together*
Galliam	*Gaul*
iter facimus	*we are making a trip*
nostra	*our*
nova	*new*
respondit	*(she) answered*
tuus	*your*
prōcūrātor Augustī	*Augustus' finance officer, procurator*
Gallī	*the Gauls*
in silvā	*in the forest*
Germānī	*the Germans*
quod	*because*
barbarī	*barbarians*
vīllās	*big houses*
in oppidīs	*in the towns*
habitant	*(they) live in*
procul	*far*
habeō	*(I) have*

ibi	*there*
laeta	*happy*
et	*too, also*
dīxit sibi	*(she) said to herself*

PATTERNS

1 Study the following sentences:

1 Celtillus clāmōrem audīvit.
Celtillus heard the shout.
2 Celtillus fūgit.
Celtillus ran away.
3 Celtillus, postquam clāmōrem audīvit, fūgit.
Celtillus, after he heard the shout, ran away.
Or: *After Celtillus heard the shout, he ran away.*
4 Celtillus erat Gallus.
Celtillus was a Gaul.
5 Rōmānī Celtillum verberāvērunt.
The Romans whipped Celtillus.
6 Rōmānī Celtillum, quod erat Gallus, verberāvērunt.
The Romans whipped Celtillus because he was a Gaul.

2 Translate the following sentences:

1 servī, quod Sāturnālia celebrābant, in triclīniō recumbēbant.
2 Lūcīlius et Gāius, postquam Iūnia cēnam parāvit, triclīnium intrāvērunt.
3 puerī, quod servī nōn labōrābant, serviēbant.
4 Cernunnus, postquam fortiter clāmāvit, Vercingetorigem laudāvit.

Key Words

1

nouns (singular) subjects	adjectives (singular)	adverb	nouns (plural) direct objects	verbs (singular) perfect tense
dux	perfidus	diū	ducēs	comprehendit
mīles	Rōmānus		mīlitēs	verberāvit
victor	stultus		victōrēs	vexāvit

2 Derivatives: duke, militia, romance, stultify, vexatious, victory.

Complete Word Meanings

Nouns and adjectives are usually listed in their nominative form (singular or plural). Third declension nouns, however, are listed with both nominative and accusative singular forms.

Verbs are usually listed in the third person singular or plural forms of the present tense. Third person singular forms of the perfect tense are given when they appear in the stories.

Ablative forms are listed after the prepositions which govern them.

Words with asterisks (*) are Key Words.

a

ā Gādibus   *from Gades*
accidit   *happens*
ad   *to*
adiuvat   *helps, is helping*
adolēscunt   *(they) grow up*
advenit   *arrives*
Aegyptius   *of Egypt, from Egypt, Egyptian*
affīgit   *fastens*
Africa   *Africa*
agit   *drives, is driving; does*
Alesia   *Alesia*
Alesiēnsēs   *of Alesia, Alesian*
aliēnī   *foreigners*
aliī   *other (plural); the others*
alter   *another, a second*
alumna   *foster daughter*
amat   *is in love with*
ambō   *both*
*ambulat   *walks, is walking; going to walk*
amīcus   *friend*
amita   *father's sister, (paternal) aunt*
amphitheātrum   *amphitheater*
*amphora   *storage jar, amphora*
Amūlius   *Amulius*
*ancilla   *slave woman*
annuit   *nods toward, agrees*
appropinquat   *approaches, comes near*
apud imperātōrem Augustum   *at the house of the Emperor Augustus*
aqua   *water*
arbor: arborem   *tree*
arēna   *arena*
Arminius   *Arminius*
arroganter   *arrogantly*
asinus   *an ass*
assentit   *agrees*
ātrium   *reception room, atrium*
*attonitus   *surprised*
audax   *daring*

*audit   *hears, listens to:* audīvit
Augusta Trēverōrum   *Augusta Treverorum*
Augustāna   *of Augustus*
aureus   *made of gold, gold(en)*
Aventīnus   *Aventine*
avunculus   *mother's brother, (maternal) uncle*
avus   *grandfather*

b

balbūtit   *stutters*
barbarus   *a, the barbarian*
benevolus   *kind*
bēstia   *beast*
bibit   *drinks, is drinking*
biceps: bicipitem   *two-headed*
bonus   *good*
bovēs   *cattle*
bulla   *a protective charm, bulla*

c

Cācus   *Cacus*
caelum   *sky, heaven*
Caesar Augustus   *Caesar Augustus*
caldus   *hot*
canis: canem   *dog*
canistrum   *basket*
cantat   *sings, is singing*
capit   *takes, grabs*
Capitōlīnus   *on the Capitoline hill*
carcer: carcerem   *prison*
*casa   *hut*
casa Remī   *Remus' hut*
casa Rōmulī   *Romulus' hut*
cauda   *tail*
celebrābat   *was celebrating*
cēna   *dinner*
cēnāvit   *ate dinner*
charta   *a sheet of papyrus, a piece of paper*
circum collum   *around his neck*
circumspectat   *looks around*

clādēs *disaster*
*clāmat *shouts:* clāmāvit
clāmor: clāmōrem *a, the shout*
claudicat *is lame, limps*
collis: collem *hill*
*comprehendit *arrests, grabs:* comprehendit
condunt *(they) found, establish*
contendunt *(they) hurry*
continet *contains*
*cōnscendit *climbs*
cōnsūmit *devours, eats*
cubiculum *bedroom*
culīna *kitchen*
cum bovibus *with the cattle*
cum familiā *with his family*
cum mustēlā *with the ferret*
cūr? *why?*
cūrat *takes care of*
currit *runs, is running*
custōs *a, the guard*

d

deinde *next, then*
*deus *god*
dē *about*
dēcurrunt *are on parade*
dēicit *throws down*
dēmulcet *strokes, pets*
dēnique *finally*
dērīdet *makes fun of*
dēscendit *gets down*
dēsunt *(they) are missing*
*dīcit *says*
dīcit sibi *says to him/herself:* dīxit sibi
difficulter *with difficulty*
discipulus *student*
discit *learns*
*diū *for a long time*
dīxit sibi *said to him/herself*
*dominus *owner, lord*
domum *home(wards)*
*domus *house*
*dormit *sleeps, is sleeping*
*dūcit *leads*
duo *two*
dūrat *has endured, lasted*
*dux *leader*

e

ē, ex *out of*
ecce! *look!*
ego *I*
ēheu! *oh dear!*
emit *buys*

emptiō *a, the purchase*
equitat *rides (a horse), is riding*
erant *(they) were*
erat *was*
ergō *therefore*
es *(you) are (singular)*
est *is*
et *and; too, also*
euge! *hurrah!*
ex Albā Longā *out of Alba Longa*
ex Britanniā *out of Britain*
ex Galliā Belgicā *out of Belgian Gaul*
exclāmat *exclaims:* exclāmāvit
exercitus *army*
exeunt *they go out*
exī! *get out!*
exit *goes out*
explicat *explains*

f

*fābula *story*
falsus *false*
familia *family*
fascinum *the "evil eye"*
ferōciter *fiercely*
fessus *tired*
festīnā! *hurry!*
festīnanter *quickly*
fīlia *daughter*
*fīlius *son*
flamma aeterna *eternal flame*
forās *outside*
*fortiter *loudly, bravely, fiercely*
forum *business center*
fossa *ditch*
*frāter *brother*
fraudābat *(he) cheated*
frīgidus *cold*
fuga *an, the escape*
fugat *chases*
fugit *escapes, runs away from*
fulget *shines*
furcifer! *scoundrel!*
*fūstis *stick*

g

Gādēs *Gades*
Gāius Rubrius Valēns *Gaius (full name of)*
Gallia *Gaul (the place)*
Gallicus *from Gaul, Gallic, Gaulish*
Gallus *a, the Gaul (the person)*
gallus *rooster*
garum *(fish-based) sauce*
geminī *twins*

gerit   *wears, is wearing*
Germānia   *Germany*
Germānicus   *in, of Germany, German*
Germānus   *a, the German*
Gēryōn   *Geryon*
*gladiātor   *gladiator*
gladius   *sword*
grātiās   *thanks*

h

*habet   *has*
habitat   *lives, lives in*
Herculēs   *Hercules*
Hispānia   *Hispania*
Hispānicus   *of Hispania, from Hispania, Hispanic*
historia   *(historical) account, story*
hodiē   *today*
horreum   *storehouse*
hortus   *garden*
humī   *on the ground*

i

iacet   *lies, is lying*
iacit   *throws*
iam diū   *now for a long time*
iānua   *door*
ibi   *there*
imperātor   *Emperor*
in   *in, into; on*
in flūmen Tiberim   *into the Tiber river*
incidit   *falls: incidit*
*īnfāns: īnfantem   *baby*
ingēns   *huge*
inimīcus   *the enemy*
inquit   *says*
īnspicit   *inspects, examines*
īnsula   *island*
intendit   *takes aim*
intentē   *intently*
*interficit   *kills*
interrogat   *questions*
*intrat   *enters: intrāvit*
invāsērunt   *(they) invaded*
invenit   *finds*
iō Sāturnālia!   *hurrah, the Saturnalia!*
*īrātus   *angry*
Ītalia   *Italy*
Ītalicus   *of Italy, from Italy, Italian*
iter facimus   *we are making a trip*
*iterum   *again*
Iūlius Caesar: Iūlium Caesarem   *Iulius [Julius] Caesar*
Iuppiter Optimus Maximus   *Jupiter the best and greatest*
iuvenis   *young man*
iūxtā   *next to, beside*

l

labōrat   *works*
*lacrimat   *cries, is crying*
laetē   *happily*
laetitia   *happiness, joy*
*laetus   *happy*
lallat   *sings, is singing a lullaby*
*latet   *lies hidden*
laudat   *praises*
lectīca   *portable couch, lectica*
lectus   *couch*
lēgātus   *a, the general*
*legiōnēs   *legions*
legit   *reads, is reading*
lentē   *slowly*
leviter   *lightly*
līber   *free*
lingua Latīna   *Latin language*
lōrum   *(leather) collar*
Lūcius Rubrius Valēns   *Lucius (full name of)*
lūdit   *plays, is playing*
lūdus   *school*
lūna   *moon*
lupa   *she-wolf*
lūstrat   *sprinkles*
lūstrātiō   *(ritual of) sprinkling*

m

*maestus   *sad*
magister   *master (of the ship), captain*
*magister   *master, teacher*
*magnus   *big*
manēbat   *(he) stayed behind*
Marcus   *Marcus*
marmoreus   *made of marble*
Mars   *Mars*
massa   *block of metal, ingot*
Massiliēnsis   *of Massilia (Marseille), from Massilia, Massilian*
*māter   *mother*
mē   *me*
mehercle!   *by Hercules!*
mēnsa   *table*
*mercātor   *merchant*
mercātus   *market*
meus   *my*
Minerva   *Minerva*
mī domine Claudī!   *my lord Claudius!*
*mīles   *soldier*
mittit   *sends*
*mortuus   *dead*
mox   *soon*
mūgītus   *the bellowing*
*multī   *many*

multum   *much, lots of*
mustēla   *ferret*

n
nārrat   *tells*
nāvem solvit   *sets sail*
nāvigat   *navigates, sails*
*nāvis: nāvem   *ship*
negōtium agō   *(I) am in business*
nepōtēs Augustī   *grandsons of Augustus*
nihil   *nothing*
nimis   *excessively, too*
nōbilis   *noble, aristocratic*
nōmen   *a, the name*
nōn   *not*
noster   *our*
novus   *new*
Numitor   *Numitor*
*nunc   *now*
nūntius   *a messenger*
*nūtrīx   *a, the nurse*

o
obstat   *blocks the way, is blocking the way*
occidentālis   *western*
ōdit   *hates*
ōhe!   *ho there!*
oi!   *oh!*
ōlim   *once (in the past)*
omnēs   *all*
omnis   *entire(ly)*
oppidum   *town*
oppidum Albam Longam   *town (of) Alba Longa*
oppugnat   *attacks*
ōrātiōnem habet   *makes a speech*
Orthus   *Orthus*
Ōstiēnsis: Ōstiēnsem   *of Ostia*

p
paedagōgus   *slave, pedagogue*
paene   *almost*
Palātīnus   *Palatine*
Palātium   *Palatine hill*
parābat   *(she) was preparing*
parit   *gives birth to*
parvus   *small*
*pater   *father*
pāstor   *shepherd*
pavīmentum   *floor*
pāx: pācem   *peace*
pellis: pellem   *a skin*
per   *through*
*perfidus   *treacherous*
perterritus   *terrified*

pestis   *pest, rascal, nuisance*
petit   *seeks, asks for, looks for*
pilleus   *a felt cap*
plaustrum   *wagon*
plēnus   *full*
pluit   *it is raining*
pōculum   *cup*
*pōnit   *puts*
*portat   *carries, is carrying*
portus   *port*
post proelium longum   *after a long battle*
*posteā   *afterwards*
postquam   *after (conjunction)*
postrīdiē   *on the next day*
praecursor: praecursōrem   *forerunner*
prior   *prior, the first*
prīnceps   *chieftain*
prō   *in front of*
prōcēdit   *advances, proceeds*
procul   *far*
prōcūrātor Augustī: prōcūrātōrem Augustī   *finance officer of Augustus, procurator*
prōcurrunt   *(they) run ahead*
proelium   *battle*
prope   *near*
publicē   *publicly*
Publius Quīntilius Vārus   *Varus (full name of)*
*puella   *girl*
*puer   *boy*
pugna   *a, the fight*
*pugnat   *fights, is fighting*
pulchra: pulchram   *beautiful*
*pulsat   *hits, knocks on: pulsāvit*
pūpa   *doll*

q
quaerit   *looks for*
quid?   *what?*
quis?   *who?*
quod   *because*
quoque   *also*

r
raeda   *(four-wheeled) carriage*
rārus   *rare*
reccidērunt   *(they) fell back, retreated*
rēctē   *correctly*
recumbit   *lies down, is lying down*
redde!   *give back!*
redūcunt   *(they) lead back*
regit   *rules*
rem...nārrat   *tells the story*
Remus   *Remus*
repellit   *repels, drives back, keeps away*

reportat *carries back*
resistēbant *(they) resisted*
*respondet *answers, replies:* respondit
retrōrsum *backwards*
Rheam *Rhea*
*rīdet *smiles*
rogat *asks*
Rōma *(city of) Rome*
Rōmae *in Rome*
Rōmānī *the Romans*
*Rōmānus *of Rome, from Rome, Roman*
Rōmulus *Romulus*
Rubrī! *Rubrius!*

s

sacrificat *sacrifices, is sacrificing*
sacrificium *a, the sacrifice*
sagitta *arrow*
*salit *jumps, is jumping*
salūtat *greets*
salūtātiō *a, the visit*
salvē! *hello!*
salvēte! *hello! (plural)*
sapiēns *wise*
Sāturnālia *the Saturnalia (festival)*
scio *(I) know*
*scrībit *writes, is writing*
scūtum *shield*
sed *but*
*sedet *sits, is sitting*
sedē! *sit!*
sedēte! *sit! (plural)*
semper *always*
senēs *old men*
servat *saves*
serviēbant *(they) were waiting (on them)*
*servus *slave*
Sextus *Sextus*
*silva *forest*
simul *together*
sīc *thus, (in) this way*
Sōl *Sun (the god)*
*sōlus *alone*
*spectat *looks at, is looking at, watches, is watching*
spectātōrēs *spectators*
spēlunca *cave*
splendidus *splendid, gleaming*
stanneus *of tin*
*stat *stands, is standing*
stilus *stylus*
strangulat *strangles*
*stultus *stupid*
*suāviter *sweetly*

*subitō *suddenly*
suit *sews, is sewing*
sum *am*
sunt *(they) are*
superāvit *(he) won*
surgit *rises, gets up*
sūrsum deorsum *up and down*
susceptiō *(ritual of) acknowledgement, acceptance*
suscipit *picks up*
synthesēs *colored robes*

t

taberna *tavern*
tabula *(waxed board) writing tablet*
*tacet *is silent, is quiet*
tamen *however*
templum *temple*
*tenet *holds, is holding*
terra *earth*
texit *weaves, is weaving*
thermae *baths*
Tiberius Claudius *Tiberius Claudius*
Titus Rubrius Valēns *Rubrius (full name of)*
toga *wool mantle worn by citizens, toga*
toga pulla *dark gray toga (mourning garment)*
trādit *hands over:* trādidit
trahit *drags*
trāns Galliam *across Gaul*
trāns Hispāniam *across Hispania*
tremit *trembles*
trēs *three*
triceps: tricipitem *three-headed*
triclīnium *dining room*
*turba *crowd*
tuus *your (singular)*
tū *you (singular)*
tūtus *safe*

u

ubi? *where?*
ubīque *everywhere*
ululāvit *(he) howled*
*urbs: urbem *city*
ut Caesar Augustus *like Caesar Augustus*
ut Germānus *like a German*
ut servī *as slaves*
ūnus *one*

v

vae! *woe!*
valdē *much, very, very much, a lot*
valē! *goodbye! (singular)*
valēte! *goodbye! (plural)*

vāgit *cries, is crying*
Vāre! *Varus!*
via *street*
venēfica *hag, witch*
veniam petit *asks for forgiveness*
venit *comes*
*verberat *whips:* verberāvit
Vercingetorix *Vercingetorix*
vēnāticus *for hunting*
*verna *slave (born in master's house)*
vertit *turns*
vexat *annoys, is annoying*
vibrat *waves, wags*
vīcīnus *neighboring; a, the neighbor*
*victōrēs *the winners*

victus *beaten*
*videt *sees*
vīlla *big house*
vīnum *wine*
vir *man*
virgō: virginem *virgin*
virgō Vestālis *Vestal Virgin*
virī *men*
vīsitā! *visit! (singular)*
*vīsitat *visits*
vīsitāte! *visit! (plural)*
vīvus *alive*
vōs *you (plural)*
vulnerātus *wounded*

Guide to Persons, Places, and Events

Boldface number(s) in brackets refers to Chapter Number, followed by Story Number(s). For example, the entry (I.2) refers to Chapter One, Story Two: **sacrificium**.

Persons marked with two asterisks (**) are fictional. Persons and places marked with one asterisk (*) are legendary (some of them may be historical). All other persons and places are historical.

*Alba Longa Town in Italy; second capital of the people later called the Romans; founded by Aeneas' son Ascanius (V.28).

*Amūlius Usurping king of Alba Longa; brother of Numitor (V.28).

Arminius Hermann (in modern German), a chieftain of the Germanic tribespeople called the Cherusci. In A.D. 9, Arminius led the destructive surprise attack on the three Roman legions commanded by Varus (IV.22,24).

Augusta Trēverōrum Augusta "of the Treveri tribespeople," an ancient city in northeastern Gaul (now Trier in modern Germany). In Augustus' time, it was the seat of his finance officer (*procūrātor*) for the three provinces called Belgian Gaul, Upper Germany, and Lower Germany (IV.22).

Augustus (*full name:* Gāius Iūlius Caesar Octāviānus Augustus) Adopted son of the celebrated Roman general, Caesar; first Emperor of Rome, 29 B.C.–A.D. 14 (III.15–16; IV.25).

*Cācus Monstrous fire-breathing beast; son of the god Vulcan. Cacus is said to have lived in a cave on the Aventine hill, one of the seven hills of Rome (III.19).

Caesar (*full name:* Gāius Iūlius Caesar) Roman general and governor, in 58–49 B.C., of the province then called Transalpine Gaul (modern France). Caesar fought many battles against the defiant Gaulish rebels and eventually subdued the province enough to allow peaceful settlement for many centuries (VI.31).

Capitōlium One of the seven hills of Rome; location of the main temple of Rome's highest patron god, Iupiter Optimus Maximus (IV.25).

**Celtillus An adult slave, born in Gaul; belonged to Rubrius (I, II, III, and VI.1,9, 15–16, 30–2).

**Cernunnus An eight-year-old slave-boy (*verna*), born in Rubrius' household; son of Celtillus and a slave mother who does not appear in the story (I–VI.1, 5, 9, 15, 16, 17, 18, 21, 25, 26, 27, 28, 29, 30, 31, 32).

Claudius (*full name:* Tiberius Claudius Nērō Germānicus) Fourth Emperor of Rome (ruled A.D. 41–54). At the time of this story (A.D. 9), Claudius was about 19 years old. Because of a speech impediment and other handicaps, he was a somewhat lonely young man. Claudius was also a scholar, and was very interested in Roman tradition and history (III, V.16, 27–9).

Gādēs An ancient city in southwestern Spain (modern Cádiz) (III.19).

Gallia Gaul, the region of western Europe now known as France; formerly a Roman province subdued by Iulius Caesar. In Augustus' time, the larger part of Transalpine Gaul was subdivided into three provinces called the Belgian, Lugdunensian, and Aquitanian Gauls (**VI**.33).

Gāius   The eight-year-old son of Rubrius and Iunia (I–VI**.1, 2, 3, 5, 6, 7, 9, 18, 25, 26, 27, 29, 31, 32).

Germānia   Germany; the Rhine river region of what is now known as Germany was divided by Augustus into two provinces called Upper and Lower Germany (**IV**.21–4).

*Gēryōn   The three-headed monster living on western Red Island; owner of an exceptionally fine herd of cattle (**III**.19).

*Herculēs   Mighty Greek demigod, son of the god Jupiter and the mortal princess Alcmena. After completing twelve labors and suffering a painful death, Hercules became a full god on Olympus (**III**.18).

Hispānia   Hispania. In Augustus' time, the Celtiberian peninsula (now shared by Portugal and Spain) was divided into three provinces called Baetica, Tarraconensian Spain, and Lusitania (**III**.19–20).

Iūnia   Wife of Rubrius; mother of Lucius, Gaius, and Rubria (I–IV, VI**.1, 2, 4, 18, 21, 32, 33).

Lugdūnum   Capital of the "Three Gauls," the newest provinces of Gaul (see **Gallia** above), now the modern city of Lyon, France; located at the meeting-point of the Rhône and Saône rivers (**VI**.33).

Lūcius   The teenaged son of Rubrius and Iunia (I, III, V–VI**.1, 2, 15, 17, 27, 32, 33).

Lūcīlia   The 12-year-old foster daughter (*alumna*) of Rubrius and Iunia (I–III, VI**.1, 2, 4, 5, 6, 7, 10, 12, 13, 19, 33).

Marcus   One of two Roman survivors from Varus' German disaster in the Teutoburg Forest (near modern Detmold, Germany) in A.D. 9 (IV**.22).

*Mars   The ancient Roman god of agriculture and war; son of Juno; father, by Rhea, of Romulus and Remus (**V**.28).

Massilia   A city port in southern Gaul (modern Marseille, France), located near the mouth of the Rhône river; originally founded by Greek colonists (**III**.14).

nepōtēs Augustī   The grandsons of Augustus, Gaius Caesar and Lucius Caesar; they were his heirs until they died as young men. Lucius died in A.D. 2 in Massilia, on his way to Spain. Gaius died in A.D. 4 in Lycia, on his way home from the East. They were the sons of Augustus' daughter Iulia and his lieutenant Marcus Agrippa (**V**.27).

*Numitor   Rightful king of Alba Longa; brother of Amulius (**V**.28).

*Orthus   The monstrous two-headed dog that guarded Geryon's cattle; son of Typhon and the snake-legged monster Echidna (**III**.19).

*Remus   Son of Mars and Rhea; grandson of Numitor; the bad twin whom Romulus killed (**V**.28–9).

*Rhea   Daughter of Numitor; mother, by Mars, of Romulus and Remus (**V**.28–9).

Rōma   Rome, city in central Italy, founded in 753 B.C.; capital of the Roman Republic and, later (after Augustus), of the Roman Empire. Still capital of modern Italy, Rome is one of the oldest and grandest continually inhabited cities in the world (**I–III**.13–18; **IV**.21–2, 26; **V–VI**).

*Rōmulus   Son of Mars and Rhea; grandson of Numitor; the good twin who founded Rome (**V**.28–9).

Rubria   Baby daughter of Rubrius and Iunia; named and ritually sprinkled by Rubrius (II, VI**.11, 33).

Rubrius   Roman businessman, with house on the Quirinal hill of Rome; member of the class of wealthy non-politicians called *equitēs*; had business interests in Gaul (France) and Hispania (Portugal and Spain). Later in A.D. 9, Rubrius was appointed finance agent (*prōcūrātor*) of the Roman province called Lugdunensian Gaul by Emperor Augustus. Rubrius and his family moved to the province's capital, Lugdunum (modern Lyon, France) (I–VI**.1, 2, 8, 10, 11, 14, 15, 16, 17, 21, 25, 26, 27, 32, 33).

Sāturnālia   The happiest of all the Roman festivals. Each year, it began on December 17 and lasted several days. Slaves and masters were allowed to reverse their customary roles and privileges. Small gifts like candles and dolls were exchanged (**VI**.30, 32–3).

Sextus   One of two Roman survivors from Varus' German disaster in the Teutoburg Forest (near modern Detmold, Germany) in A.D. 9 (IV**.22).

*Sōl   Sun, the god who drove the solar chariot; son of the Titan gods Hyperion and Theia (**III**.19).

Specla   Old slave woman, born in Hispania; belonged to Rubrius; nurse to Lucius, Gaius, and Rubria (I–III, VI**.1, 4, 10, 12, 13, 18, 19, 30).

Vārus (*full name*: Publius Quīntilius Vārus)   Commander of the Roman army that Arminius and his German soldiers destroyed in the Teutoburg Forest in northern Germany in A.D. 9 (**IV**.21, 24).

Vercingetorix   Chieftain of the Gaulish tribespeople called the Arverni; led an alliance of Gaulish tribes and towns against Caesar and the Romans in 52 B.C. After the surrender of Alesia, where Vercingetorix had made his last stand, he was handed over by the town's elders to Caesar. Vercingetorix was later displayed in Caesar's victory parade, and eventually executed (**VI**.31–2).

virgō Vestālis   Vestal Virgin, a priestess of the hearth-goddess Vesta. The Vestal Virgins were expected to live by strict rules, segregated from men (**V**.28).

Guide to Word Patterns

Boldface numbers refer to Chapter Number, followed by the Story Number after which the Pattern is described. For example, the entry (**I.2**) refers to Chapter One, Story Two: **sacrificium**.

The boldface letter **E** refers to the inside of the back End Cover, followed by the Section Number. So, for example, the entry (**E.1**) refers to the inside of the back End Cover, Section 1 (**Nouns**).

"a" and "the" (lack of) **I.2**

adverbs (undeclined) **III.18**

call-out names (vocatives) **III.19 and 23; E.1**

commands (singular and plural) **III.19; E.2**

-ērunt perfect tense verb ending (3rd person plural) **VI.32; E.2**

-it perfect tense verb ending (3rd person singular) **VI.32; E.2**

-m noun ending (accusative singular) **II.7; E.1**

-m noun ending for direct object **II.7; E.1**

-nt imperfect tense verb ending (3rd person plural) **VI.32; E.2**

-nt verb ending (3rd person plural) **IV.23; E.2**

-ō verb ending (1st person singular) **V.28; E.2**

postquam "after" with subordinate clause (conjunction) **VI.34**

quod "because" in subordinate clause (conjunction) **VI.34**

-s verb ending (2nd person singular) **V.28; E.2**

-t imperfect tense verb ending (3rd person singular) **VI.32; E.2**

-t verb ending (3rd person singular) **I.3; E.2**

-t verb ending translated with "she," "he," or "it" **II.8; E.2**

two verbs, with single subject, connected by **et** **II.11**

verbs of saying (position of) **III.15**

vocative noun-forms **III.19 and 23; E.1**